English-to-Japanese Interpreting 101

English-to-Japanese Interpreting 101

Fundamentals of Broadcast, Consecutive, and Simultaneous Interpretation

John McLean

MATATABI PRESS

Typesetting and design copyright © MATATABI PRESS (910554), a subdivision of MATATABI HOLDINGS. No part of this book may be reproduced or transmitted in any form or by any means, electronic or mechanical, including photocopying, recording, or by any information storage and retrieval system, without permission in writing from the publisher.

First Printing, July 2024

MATATABI PRESS (910554)
Windwhistle, Farley Hill, Matlock. DE4 3LL. UK
20-20, 5-Chome, Yamamoto-shinmachi, Asaminami-ku, Hiroshima. 731-0139. JAPAN
https://www.press.matatabi-japan.com/
https://www.holdings.matatabi-japan.com/
Email: press@matatabi-japan.com
Tel: 0081-(0)70-8592-2501

CONTENTS

CONTENTS

This 15-week **English-to-Japanese Interpreter Training Course/ Textbook** employs a group work approach to develop various interpreting strategies relevant to a wide range of working environments. Using a constructivist pedagogical approach, this course assists trainee interpreters in developing a deep understanding of each strategy, including its limitations and alternatives, while establishing a solid foundation in the fundamental knowledge of the field.

Course Objectives

This course is designed to:

(1) **Develop core English-to-Japanese interpreting skills,** including:

- Broadcast Interpreting
- Consecutive Interpreting (Memory)
- Consecutive Interpreting (Note-taking)
- Sight Translation
- Simultaneous Interpreting

(2) **Refine Understanding of the Interpreting Field and Elevate English Presentation Skills** by crafting presentations on:

- History of Interpreting in Japan
- Eight Types of Interpreters
- Translation and Interpreting Technologies

- Interpreter Training Techniques
- Companies/Organizations Recruiting Interpreters
- Companies/Organizations Recruiting English-Language Specialists
- Interpreter Qualifications
- Professional and Academic Interpreter Associations
- Interpreting Roles at International Film/Animation Festivals

Also Included in This Edition

(1) **12 Tried-and-tested Tips for Effective Interpreting**
(2) **5 Tips for Communication**
(3) **4 Voice Training Techniques**
(4) **12 Strategies for Enhancing Your Sight Translation Skills**
(5) **7 Short Talks** packed with information on:

- Translation Technology
- Effectiveness of Prosody and Content Shadowing
- Chiune Sugihara, the Japanese Linguist Who Defied the Nazis
- When and Where Interpreters Use Sight Translation
- Interpreter Qualifications
- International Interpreter Associations
- Roles of Interpreters at International Film and Animation Festivals

(6) **QR Codes for Various Resources**, including:

- British English, American English, and Bilingual Shadowing Materials
- Technical Advice on Creating MP4 PowerPoint Video Presentations

- Guides for Conference, Medical, Legal, and Academic Translator/Interpreter Associations and Federations
- Latest CAT Tools, Machine Translation, and Interpreting Tools
- Interpreter Examinations, Qualifications, and Standards
- Film Festivals and Supporting Bodies

(7) **6 Stories by Kotaro Tanaka (1880-1941)** translated into English and adapted for consecutive interpreting activities

(8) **Glossary of 50 Core Interpreting Terms**

ADVICE: To fully benefit from this course, you will require:

- A device capable of creating and recording PowerPoint presentations
- A stable Wi-Fi connection

NOTE: Professionals often interpret both English-to-Japanese and Japanese-to-English. However, as this course is only 15 weeks long, the focus is given to English-to-Japanese interpretation.

Introduction

Three Interpreting and One Translation Mode

This course covers three interpreting modes—*broadcast*, *consecutive*, and *simultaneous*—and one translation mode—*sight*. As a professional interpreter, mastering all is essential since you may have to switch between them seamlessly in a single assignment. Here's a overview of each:

Broadcast Interpreting: Interpreters translate and then read information for TV, radio, or other media broadcasts. They usually get a script beforehand to prepare, ensuring accurate delivery by following the live broadcast.

Consecutive Interpreting: In consecutive interpreting, the interpreter interprets after the speaker pauses. This method allows for a step-by-step exchange of information, ensuring accurate interpretation.

Sight Translation: Interpreters orally translate written text on the spot, instantly conveying its meaning to an audience. This is often used in legal, medical, guide (tourism) or business settings.

Simultaneous Interpreting: Interpreters interpret the speaker's words in real-time, delivering the message instantly while the speaker continues.

This is commonly used in conferences or meetings needing immediate interpretation.

Task - Write the Japanese for the following:

1. Broadcast Interpreting: _______________________
2. Consecutive Interpreting: _______________________
3. Sight Translation: _______________________
4. Simultaneous Interpreting: _______________________

Warm-up
Consecutive Interpreting (Memory)

In interviews, discussing past experiences is common. ***Consecutive interpreting (memory),*** a vital skill for interpreters, is the ideal ideal interpreting approach for this kind of topic. Interpreters simply visualize the events described and convey them accurately in another language, similar to storytelling. Professional interpreters often employ consecutive interpreting for responses up to three minutes. That said, 60 seconds is a good starting point for trainee interpreters. The upcoming activity aims to help you hone this skill.

- In groups of two or three, take turns talking about what you did last weekend ***in English*** for about ***60 seconds*** each. (See Communication Tip 1)
- Practice active listening by visualizing your groupmate's story as he or she speaks.
- Then, recount their story ***in Japanese***, demonstrating your understanding and engagement. (See Interpreting Tips 1 and 2).

COMMUNICATION TIP 1: Include details about ***who*** you were with, ***what*** you did, ***where*** you went, ***when*** it occurred, and ***why*** it was meaningful to you.

INTERPRETING TIP 1: When recounting the story, use *first-person narrative*, employing *"I"* instead of *"he," "she,"* or *"they."* As an interpreter, it's crucial to speak as though you are the person you are interpreting for, conveying their experiences and emotions as your own.

INTERPRETING TIP 2: *Genuine Interest* — Having a genuine interest in your groupmate's experiences not only makes it easier to remember but also makes the language exchange more enjoyable and effective.

Activity 1
How Interpreters Juggle Two Languages at Once

Scan the QR code to view Ewandro Magalhaes's TED-Ed Talk *How Interpreters Juggle Two Languages at Once*, focusing on interpreters' essential role in diplomacy and the need for precise communication. After watching the video, respond to the seven questions, below.

How Interpreters Juggle Two Languages at Once
https://www.youtube.com/watch?v=cXNTArhA0Jg

Week 1 Quiz (See Appendix A for sample answers)

1) What was the mistake made by the interpreter in translating Nikita Khrushchev's words in 1956?______________________________

____
____

2) How did the incorrect translation impact the relations between the Soviet Union and the US during the Cold War?_______________

____

____

3) Why is it important to interpret conversations accurately, especially in diplomatic contexts?_______________________

____

____

4) How did interpreters usually work before the introduction of simultaneous interpretation systems?_________________

____

____

5) What is the purpose of the simultaneous interpretation system, and how is it different from the older methods?_______________

____

____

6) How do interpreters improve their language skills to become proficient conference interpreters?___________________

____

____

7) How do interpreters prepare themselves mentally to handle the stress of interpreting in high-pressure environments like the UN General Assembly?_______________________

____

____

Activity 2
Shadowing

Shadowing involves listening to a speaker and repeating their words simultaneously in the same language. As discussed in **Ewandro Magalhaes's TED-Ed Talk**, shadowing is a key skill for interpreters to practice accurate message delivery across languages in conferences. This activity aims to enhance your English shadowing ability.

1. Scan the QR code, below, to access the **BBC Learning English - 6 Minute English** website.
2. Search the site for a topic that interests you.
3. Open the video and scroll down to the its script.
4. Play the while reading the script simultaneously.
5. Focus on imitating the speakers' rhythm and intonation as you listen and read.
6. Once you feel comfortable, repeat this process without the script.
7. Practice this method repeatedly until you can shadow the full 6 minutes.

BBC Learning English - 6 Minute English
https://www.bbc.co.uk/learningenglish/english/features/
6-minute-english

Preparation for Week 2

Task 1: Shadowing

Try to develop a habit of shadowing, with and/or without a script, for 10 to 15 minutes a day. Feel free to use the talks on the **BBC Learning English** website or any other English language materials you have an interest in.

Task 2: 90-Second English PowerPoint Presentation (See Appendix B for a sample presentation)

Create a 90-second PowerPoint presentation in English about the ***history of interpreting in Japan***.

Interpreting in Japan has a rich history dating back centuries, playing a vital role in facilitating communication with other countries during trade, diplomacy, and cultural exchanges. Feel free to explore various topics on interpreting history in Japan in your presentation, such as:

(1) ***Ancient Roots***: Interpreters helped bridge communication gaps between Japan and other nations, shaping early trade and cultural exchanges.

(2) ***Classical Period***: Court interpreters translated Chinese texts, influencing Japanese language, culture, and writing systems.

(3) ***Feudal Japan***: Interpreters were vital for diplomacy and trade, particularly with China and Korea. Portuguese and Dutch traders and missionaries in the 16th and 17th centuries increased the demand for interpreters, facilitating trade and knowledge exchange between Japan and the Western world amid growing international interactions.

(4) ***Modernization***: Japan's increased engagement with the West in the late 19th century led to a greater need for interpreters in international diplomacy and trade agreements.

(5) ***Post-World War II***: The demand for interpreters surged after World War II to support international business, political negotiations, and foreign interactions.

(6) ***Technological Advancements***: Recent technological advances have revolutionized interpreting in Japan, introducing devices, video conferencing, and remote services.

(7) ***Specialized Fields***: Interpreting in Japan now covers legal, medical, conference, business, and media fields, reflecting the country's growing global presence.

Record and export your presentation in .mp4 format for file sharing with your classmates in Week 2. The .mp4 format is widely compatible with different devices. For guidance on this process, scan the QR code provided below.

The Presentation University
https://www.youtube.com/watch?v=pIV0SC7QeM8

Task 3: English Script and Short Bilingual Vocabulary List

Prepare an English script in .docx or .pdf format for your PowerPoint presentation, along with a bilingual list (English and Japanese) of key vocabulary from your presentation. Your classmates will use your script and vocabulary list to prepare a Japanese translation of your presentation for their ***broadcast interpretation*** tasks in Week 2.

History of Interpreting in Japan

Warm-up 1
Consecutive Interpreting (Memory)

In this week's ***consecutive interpreting (memory)*** exercise, you'll have an additional 10 seconds to enhance your performance. Before beginning, familiarize yourself with ***Communication Tip 2*** and ***Interpreting Tip 3*** provided below.

1. In groups of two or three, take turns talking about what you did last weekend ***in English*** for about <u>***70 seconds***</u> each.
2. Practice active listening by visualizing your groupmate's story as he or she speaks.
3. Then, recount their story ***in Japanese***, demonstrating your understanding and engagement.
4. **IMPORTANT**: Use first-person narrative, employing "I" instead of "he" or "she."

COMMUNICATION TIP 2: Use transitional language to smoothly link parts of your story, helping listeners follow the narrative.

- Introducing Background: ***Before this happened...*** or ***To give you a bit of background...***

- Moving to a Significant Moment: *The turning point was...* or *That's when things changed...*
- Highlighting Results: *As a result...* or *Consequently...*
- Adding Details: *In addition...* or *Furthermore...*
- Concluding: *In the end...* or *Looking back...*

INTERPRETING TIP 3: *Encourage Feedback* — After recounting the story, encourage your groupmate(s) to provide feedback on your interpretation. This constructive feedback can be invaluable for improving both your linguistic skills and your ability to convey stories effectively.

Warm-up 2
Shadowing

Building on what you did last week, in this week's shadowing practice, you're going to pick another 6-minute English program to practice.

1. Access the **BBC Learning English - 6 Minute English** website using the QR code provided below.
2. Choose a program of interest, read its script while listening, focusing on mimicking the speakers' rhythm and intonation.
3. Practice shadowing the program without the script repeatedly until you can shadow the full 6 minutes.

BBC Learning English - 6 Minute English
https://www.bbc.co.uk/learningenglish/english/features/
6-minute-english

Activity 1
Broadcast Interpreting

This activity is designed to replicate the exacting demands of **broadcast interpreting**. Interpreters in this field usually receive a speech or presentation script at least a day in advance. They meticulously translate or annotate the script and rehearse reading it to synchronize with the speed and cadence of the original speaker. Despite sometimes being held to much tighter deadlines, including receiving materials less than an hour before interpreting, interpreters must still maintain peak performance quality. This demand to excel under stringent deadlines encapsulates the professional realm of **broadcast interpreting**, a trial that you will confront through this activity.

Part 1: Transcript Preparation (10 Minutes)

1. Form groups of 2 to 4 members and exchange your English scripts and bilingual vocabulary lists about the **history of interpreting in Japan**.
2. Use the provided space, below, to translate the script into Japanese.
3. **IMPORTANT**: Don't use dictionaries or online resources during this exercise. The goal is to deeply consider what each English sentence conveys and to translate it into Japanese as naturally as possible. If any words or phrases are unclear, feel free to ask the groupmate who wrote the script for further explanation.

____

____

____

____

____

____

Part 2: Preparing Your Voice 1 (3 Minutes - Lip Trills)

Enhancing vocal ***clarity***, ***articulation***, ***projection***, and overall delivery is crucial for broadcast interpreters. ***Voice training*** plays a vital role in achieving these goals. These exercises not only help interpreters to communicate effectively and engage their audience but also aid in preventing vocal strain during prolonged interpreting sessions.

1. Stand up straight or sit comfortably with good posture.
2. Relax your facial muscles, jaw, and lips.
3. Take a deep breath in through your nose.
4. Exhale slowly through your lips while making a "brrr" or "brrrrr" sound like you're rolling your Rs.
5. Feel the vibrations in your lips and around your face while doing the trill.
6. Repeat this exercise for 2-3 minutes to warm up your voice and improve vocal flexibility.

Part 3: Broadcast Interpreting Practice (5 Minutes)

Having warmed up your voice and enhanced your vocal flexibility, it's time to practice broadcast interpreting with your groupmate's presentation on the ***history of interpreting in Japan***. Exchange .mp4 files within your group, play the video, and articulate your Japanese script to synchronize with the English audio. The shadowing practice that you have been doing should help you to be comfortable listening and speaking at the same time. Maintain composure and aim for clear, audible delivery. Repeat this process as many times as possible within the allotted five-minute timeframe.

NOTE: Many of the interpreting tips mentioned in the ***Consecutive Interpreting (Memory)*** warm-ups can also be applied to broadcast interpreting.

Part 4: Broadcast Interpreting Performance

Conduct your broadcast interpreting performance within your group, ensuring that everyone has clear visibility of the PowerPoint .mp4 presentation. While listening to your classmate's interpretation, note areas for potential improvement using the following table.

Evaluation Criteria	Rating (1-5)	Comments
Accuracy		Alignment with the original message
Clarity		Clarity of message delivery
Pronunciation		Pronunciation accuracy and clarity
Tone & Intonation		Matching speaker's tone and intonation
Pacing		Interpretation speed and flow
Confidence		Presenter's confidence and composure
Overall Performance		Overall interpretation evaluation

Activity 2
Broadcast Interpreting

If time allows, exchange files with another group member and repeat Parts 1, 3 and 4.

Preparation for Week 3

Task 1: Shadowing

Once again, work on developing a habit of shadowing, with and/or without a script, for 10 to 15 minutes a day. Feel free to use the talks on the **BBC Learning English** website or any other English language materials you have an interest in. Developing consistent habits like shadowing may take some time, but the benefits, such as improved language fluency and pronunciation, will be well worth the effort.

Task 2: 2-Minute English PowerPoint Presentation

Create a *2-minute* PowerPoint presentation in English about one of the four following *types of interpreter*:

(1) *Conference Interpreter*: Conference interpreters specialize in interpreting during conferences, seminars, and other large-scale events. They work in different modes like simultaneous interpretation (interpreting in real-time) or consecutive interpretation (waiting for speakers to finish before interpreting).

(2) *Broadcast Interpreter*: Broadcast interpreters work in the television or radio industry, providing real-time interpretation for live broadcasts, news programs, interviews, and other media content. They ensure that the audience receives accurate and timely interpretation of spoken content.

(3) *Public Service Interpreter (Police)*: Public service interpreters working with police departments provide language support in legal settings such as police interviews, court proceedings, and other law enforcement interactions where individuals require language assistance. They play a critical role in ensuring effective communication and due process.

(4) ***Business Interpreter***: Business interpreters specialize in interpreting within corporate settings, such as meetings, negotiations, presentations, and other business-related interactions. They help facilitate communication between international clients, employees, and stakeholders to ensure smooth business operations and effective collaboration.

Record and export your presentation in .mp4 format for file sharing with your classmates in Week 3.

Task 3: English Script and Short Bilingual Vocabulary List

Create an English script (.docx or .pdf) and a bilingual key vocabulary list (English and Japanese) for your PowerPoint presentation. Your classmates will use these materials to prepare a Japanese translation of your presentation for Week 3 broadcast interpretation tasks.

Types of Interpreter (1)

Warm-up 1
Consecutive Interpreting (Memory)

This week, improve your *consecutive interpreting (memory)* exercise with an extra 10 seconds. Review and apply *Communication Tip 3* and *Interpreting Tip 4* before you start.

1. In groups of two or three, take turns talking about what you did last weekend *in English* for about *80 seconds* each.
2. Visualize your groupmate's story as you listen.
3. Retell their story in Japanese using first-person narrative ("I" instead of "he/she").

COMMUNICATION TIP 3: Incorporate sensory elements like *sight, sound, smell, taste,* and *touch* to make your narrative vivid and engaging for the listener(s).

- Sight: *Saw, watched, observed*
- Sound: *Heard, listened*
- Smell: *Smelled*
- Taste: *Savored, sampled, tasted*
- Touch: *Felt, touched*

INTERPRETING TIP 4: *Practice Emotional Matching* — Try to match the tone and emotion of your groupmate when recounting their story. If they were excited about something, convey that excitement through your voice and expressions.

Warm-up 2
Shadowing

For this week's shadowing, follow these steps:

1. Use the provided QR code, below, to access the **BBC Learning English - 6 Minute English** website.
2. Select a program, listen and read along, imitate the rhythm and intonation.
3. Practice shadowing without the script until you can do all 6 minutes.

BBC Learning English - 6 Minute English
https://www.bbc.co.uk/learningenglish/english/features/
6-minute-english

Task - Write the Japanese for the following:

1. Conference Interpreter: _________________________
2. Broadcast Interpreter: _________________________
3. Public Service Interpreter (Police): _________________________
4. Business Interpreter: _________________________

Activity 1
Broadcast Interpreting

This activity simulates the high-pressure environment of ***broadcast interpreting***, where you will practice translating and synchronizing with a script under tight deadlines, mirroring real-world challenges.

Part 1: Transcript Preparation (10 Minutes)

1. Form groups of 2 to 4 members and exchange your English scripts and bilingual vocabulary lists about the four following types of interpreter: ***conference, broadcast, public service - police, and business.***
2. Use the provided space, below, to translate the script into Japanese.
3. **IMPORTANT**: Translate English sentences into Japanese naturally without dictionaries or online resources; ask the script provider for clarifications if needed.

Part 2: Preparing Your Voice 2 (4 Minutes - Humming)

Developing *resonance and control* in your voice contributes significantly to your interpreting performance. This exercise focuses on enhancing the depth and warmth of your voice, ensuring your message comes across clearly and engagingly.

1. Sit or stand comfortably, maintaining good posture.
2. Relax your shoulders, jaw, and facial muscles.
3. Inhale deeply through your nose.
4. Exhale slowly while producing a humming sound like "mmm" or "mmmmm" to feel vibrations in your chest and throat.
5. Focus on the resonance in your voice and the vibrations as you hum.
6. Repeat this exercise for 3-4 minutes to strengthen your voice resonance and improve vocal control.

Part 3: Broadcast Interpreting Practice (5 Minutes)

Apply your improved voice skills to practice broadcast interpreting with your groupmate's presentation on one or more of the four following interpreter types: *conference, broadcast, public service (police), and business*. Exchange .mp4 files, synchronize your Japanese script with the English audio, focusing on clear, audible delivery within a five-minute timeframe. Repeat as often as possible.

Part 4: Broadcast Interpreting Performance

Present your broadcast interpretation to the group, ensuring all can view the PowerPoint .mp4. Take notes on each classmate's performance for improvement using the provided table.

Evaluation Criteria	Rating (1-5)	Comments
Accuracy		Alignment with the original message
Clarity		Clarity of message delivery
Pronunciation		Pronunciation accuracy and clarity
Tone & Intonation		Matching speaker's tone and intonation
Pacing		Interpretation speed and flow
Confidence		Presenter's confidence and composure
Overall Performance		Overall interpretation evaluation

Activity 2
Broadcast Interpreting

If time allows, exchange files with another group member and repeat Parts 1, 3 and 4.

Preparation for Week 4

Task 1: Shadowing

Practice shadowing daily for 10-15 minutes, using materials like those on the **BBC Learning English** website. Consistent shadowing habits will enhance language fluency and pronunciation.

Task 2: 3-Minute English PowerPoint Presentation

Create a *3-minute* PowerPoint presentation in English about one of the four following *types of interpreter*:

(1) *Guide Interpreter*: Guide Interpreters specialize in providing interpretation services for tourists and visitors. They accompany individuals or groups and help bridge the language barrier by interpreting conversations, explanations, and other information related to the places being visited. For more information, use the QR code, below, to access the Hiroshima Interpreter & Guide Association website.

Hiroshima Interpreter and Guide Association
https://j-higa.net/

(2) *Sports Interpreter*: Sports Interpreters work within the sports industry, providing interpretation services for athletes, coaches, officials, and other personnel involved in sports events. They ensure

effective communication in various sports-related contexts such as interviews, press conferences, and team meetings.

(3) *Public Service Interpreter (Hospitals)*: Public Service Interpreters in hospitals specialize in facilitating communication between health-care providers and patients who have limited proficiency in the local language. They play a crucial role in ensuring accurate and empathetic communication during medical consultations, treatments, and other healthcare interactions. For more information, use the QR code, below, to access the Medical Interpreting Association of Japan website.

Medical Interpreting Association of Japan
https://www.imiaweb-japan.net/

(4) *Volunteer Interpreter*: Volunteer Interpreters offer their interpreting services on a voluntary basis without financial compensation. They may work in various settings such as community events, non-profit organizations, schools, or during times of crisis to assist individuals who require language support but may not have the means to hire a professional interpreter.

Record and export your presentation in .mp4 format for file sharing with your classmates in Week 4.

Task 3: English Script and Short Bilingual Vocabulary List

Create an English script (.docx or .pdf) and a bilingual key vocabulary list (English and Japanese) for your PowerPoint presentation. Your classmates will use these materials to prepare a Japanese translation of your presentation for Week 4 broadcast interpretation tasks.

Types of Interpreter (2)

Warm-up 1
Consecutive Interpreting (Memory)

This week, improve your *consecutive interpreting (memory)* exercise with an additional 10 seconds. Review and apply *Communication Tip 4* and *Interpreting Tip 5* before you start.

1. In groups of two or three, take turns talking about what you did last weekend *in English* for about **_90 seconds_** each.
2. Visualize your groupmate's story as you listen.
3. Retell their story in Japanese using first-person narrative ("I" instead of "he/she").

COMMUNICATION TIP 4: *Prioritize Key Events* — If the story is complex or contains many events, focus on the most crucial points to keep the retelling concise and impactful.

INTERPRETING TIP 5: *Simplify If Needed* — If you find certain parts of the story complex to interpret directly, it's okay to simplify these elements. The goal is to convey the essence and emotion of the story, ensuring understanding remains clear.

Warm-up 2
Shadowing

For this week's shadowing, follow these steps:

1. Use the provided QR code, below, to access the **BBC Learning English - 6 Minute English** website.
2. Select a program, listen and read along, imitate the rhythm and intonation.
3. Practice shadowing without the script until you can do all 6 minutes.

BBC Learning
English

Task - Write the Japanese for the following:

1. Guide Interpreter: ______________________
2. Sports Interpreter: ______________________
3. Public Service Interpreter (Hospitals): ________________________
4. Volunteer Interpreter: ____________________

Activity 1
Broadcast Interpreting

This activity simulates the high-pressure environment of ***broadcast interpreting***, where you will practice translating and synchronizing with a script under tight deadlines, mirroring real-world challenges.

Part 1: Transcript Preparation (10 Minutes)

1. In groups of 2 to 4 exchange your English scripts and bilingual vocabulary lists about the four following types of interpreter: *guide, sports, public service - hospitals, and volunteer.*
2. Use the provided space, below, to translate the script into Japanese.
3. **IMPORTANT**: Don't use dictionaries or online resources; ask the script provider for clarifications if needed.

Part 2: Preparing Your Voice 3 (5 Minutes - Facial Flexibility)

Enhancing *facial muscle flexibility and articulation* is vital in improving interpreting performance. This exercise, involving holding a pen in your mouth while reading aloud, helps *enhance articulation*, ensuring *clearer and more engaging communication*.

1. Sit or stand comfortably, maintaining good posture.
2. Hold a pen horizontally between your teeth without biting down on it, ensuring it doesn't obstruct your speech.

3. Take a deep breath in through your nose.

4. Read aloud your Japanese translation of your groupmate's script with clear articulation and precise pronunciation while holding the pen in your mouth.

5. Focus on enunciating each word accurately and projecting your voice effectively.

6. Pay attention to how the pen affects the movement of your facial muscles and articulation.

7. Repeat this exercise for 5 minutes to improve facial muscle flexibility and enhance articulation.

Part 3: Broadcast Interpreting Practice (5 Minutes)

Apply your improved voice skills to practice ***broadcast interpreting*** with your groupmate's presentation on one or more of the four following interpreter types: ***guide, sports, public service (hospitals), and volunteer***. Exchange .mp4 files, synchronize your Japanese script with the English audio, focusing on clear, audible delivery within a five-minute timeframe. Repeat as often as possible.

Part 4: Broadcast Interpreting Performance

Present your ***broadcast interpretation*** to the group, ensuring all can view the PowerPoint .mp4. Take notes on each classmate's performance for improvement using the provided table.

Evaluation Criteria	Rating (1-5)	Comments
Accuracy		Alignment with the original message
Clarity		Clarity of message delivery

Pronunciation		Pronunciation accuracy and clarity
Tone & Intonation		Matching speaker's tone and intonation
Pacing		Interpretation speed and flow
Confidence		Presenter's confidence and composure
Overall Performance		Overall interpretation evaluation

Activity 2
Broadcast Interpreting

If time allows, exchange files with another group member and repeat Parts 1, 3 and 4.

Preparation for Week 5

Task 1: Shadowing

Practice shadowing daily for 10-15 minutes, using materials like those on the **BBC Learning English** website. Consistent shadowing habits will enhance language fluency and pronunciation.

Task 2: Review

Review what you have learned over the past four weeks.

Broadcast Interpreting Review

Summary of Learning

Welcome to our first review lesson. Over the past four weeks, you have honed your skills in various aspects of interpreting:

(1) You've practiced *talking about past experiences* and *consecutively interpreting (memory)* your groupmates' descriptions of experiences.

(2) You've applied *four communication tips* to improve the quality and depth of your descriptions of past experiences.

(3) You've learned *five interpreting tips* to help you to both comprehend what you are interpreting are fully engage with your listeners.

(4) You've improved your *shadowing* abilities by engaging with six-minute topical discussions.

(5) You've created and recorded *PowerPoint presentations* on the *history of interpreting in Japan* and *eight different types of interpreter*.

(6) You've tried *three* different *voice training* activities to enhance your vocal skills in preparation for interpreting.

(7) You've delved into the world of *broadcast interpreting* through practical exercises.

In today's lesson, the focus is on:

- Reviewing and assessing the effectiveness of what you've learned.
- Engaging in a short ***broadcast interpreting*** test in front of your classmates to showcase your progress.

Learning Comprehension Check

(Write your answers in English and Japanese)

(1) What are the three types of interpretation covered in this course?__

____

____

(2) Into which different eras can the history of interpretation in Japan be divided?_______________________________________

____

____

____

____

(3) What are the eight distinct types of interpreters discussed in this course?_______________________________________

____

____

____

____

(4) Which, if any, of the eight types of interpreters are interested in specializing in and explain why?_______________________

____

____

____

____

Consecutive Interpreting (Memory) Review

You were given *five interpreting tips* to improve your *consecutive interpreting*. Use the space below to describe each tip in *Japanese*. Explain which you found to be the most effective and why.

____

____

____

____

____

____

____

____

____

____

____

____

____

____

Shadowing Review

You have used the **BBC Learning English** website to complete *four shadowing exercises*. Use the space on the following page to answer the following questions in English or Japanese:

(1) Why is it important for interpreters to practice shadowing?

(2) How frequently have you engaged in shadowing practice outside of class?

(3) Describe the materials you have used for shadowing practice outside of class.

(4) What can you do to further enhance your shadowing technique?

____

Voice Training Review

You have tried ***three different voice training techniques*** to enhance your voice for interpreting. Use the space below to describe each technique in ***Japanese***. Explain which you found to be the most effective and why.

____

____

____

____

____

____

____

Broadcast Interpreting Review

Your classmates have provided feedback on your **broadcast interpreting** in the following areas: **accuracy, clarity, pronunciation, tone & intonation, pacing, confidence**, and **overall performance**. Reflect on your progress and the feedback you have received to answer the following questions in English or Japanese:

(1) What do you consider to be your **broadcast interpreting strengths and weaknesses**?

(2) How do you intend to **enhance your broadcast interpreting** performance from now on?

____

____

____

____

____

____

____

____

____

____

____

Broadcast Interpreting Test

Part 1: Transcript Preparation (10 Minutes)

(1) Your teacher will assign you a test partner. Exchange your English scripts and bilingual vocabulary lists about the four following types of interpreter: *guide, sports, public service - hospitals, and volunteer*.

(2) Use the provided space, below, to translate the script into Japanese.

(3) **IMPORTANT**: Don't use dictionaries or online resources; ask the script provider for clarifications if needed.

____
____
____
____
____
____
____
____
____
____
____
____
____
____
____
____
____

Part 2: Preparing Your Voice 4 (5 Minutes)

Utilize any of the voice training activities introduced between Weeks 2 and 4, or the *pitch and tone variation exercise* detailed below, to prepare your voice for the broadcast interpreting performance assessment.

Pitch and Tone Variation Exercise

Refining *pitch and tone variation* skills is essential for interpreters to convey nuanced meanings and emotions, elevating audience engagement. This exercise aims to enhance vocal expressiveness and modulation for more effective and engaging interpretations.

(1) Sit or stand comfortably, maintaining good posture.

(2) Relax your facial muscles, jaw, and shoulders to release tension.

(3) Inhale deeply through your nose to fill your lungs.

(4) Exhale slowly and smoothly as you read one or two sentences of your translation of your partner's presentation script.

(5) Focus on varying your pitch and tone throughout the passage to convey different meanings or emotions.

(6) Experiment with high and low pitch variations, as well as changes in tone to emphasize certain words or phrases.

Pitch denotes the frequency of vocal sounds – higher pitch signifies urgency or excitement, while lower pitch conveys depth or seriousness.

Tone represents the emotional quality of the voice, conveying sincerity, empathy, authority, or warmth. Interpreters can enhance interpretations by modulating tone effectively, resulting in engaging and impactful message delivery.

Part 3: Broadcast Interpreting Practice (5 Minutes)

Apply your improved voice skills to practice **broadcast interpreting** with your groupmate's presentation on one or more of the four following interpreter types: **guide, sports, public service (hospitals),** and **volunteer**. Exchange .mp4 files, synchronize your Japanese script with the English audio, focusing on clear, audible delivery within a five-minute timeframe. Repeat as often as possible.

Part 4: Broadcast Interpreting Performance

Present your **broadcast interpretation** to the whole class, ensuring all can view the PowerPoint .mp4. After you finish, evaluate your performance for improvement using the following table.

Evaluation Criteria	Rating (1-5)	Comments
Accuracy		Alignment with the original message
Clarity		Clarity of message delivery
Pronunciation		Pronunciation accuracy and clarity
Tone & Intonation		Matching speaker's tone and intonation
Pacing		Interpretation speed and flow
Confidence		Presenter's confidence and composure
Overall Performance		Overall interpretation evaluation

Preparation for Week 6

Task 1: Shadowing

Practice shadowing daily for 10-15 minutes, using materials like those on the **BBC Learning English** website. Consistent shadowing habits will enhance language fluency and pronunciation.

Task 2: 3-Minute English PowerPoint Presentation

Create a *3-minute* PowerPoint presentation in English about one or more of the three following categories of *translation/interpreting technology*:

(1) *CAT Tools*: Computer-Assisted Translation (CAT) tools are software applications designed to aid translators in the translation process. These tools help improve translation efficiency, consistency, and accuracy by storing previously translated segments in a translation memory, offering terminology databases, and providing other features to facilitate the translation workflow. Here are the *top CAT tools* based on a ranking by G2:

CAT Tools Ranking
https://www.g2.com/categories/computer-assisted-translation/small-business

(2) ***Machine Translation***: Machine Translation automates text translation between languages using computer software, facilitating quick translations for instant communication and information retrieval. Here are the ***top Machine Translation*** tools based on a ranking by G2:

Translation Machine Ranking
https://www.g2.com/categories/machine-translation

(3) ***Machine Interpreting***: Machine Interpreting tools offer rapid cross-language interpretation but may struggle with nuances like human interpreters. While vital for multilingual communication, they face challenges with complex contexts and cultural nuances. Limited machine interpreting systems support Japanese-English interpretation; scan the QR code for access to one such tool (Pocketalk).

Pocketalk Interpreting Machine
https://pocketalk.jp/

Record and export your presentation in .mp4 format for file sharing with your classmates in Week 6.

Task 3: Short Bilingual Vocabulary List

Generate a bilingual (English and Japanese) key vocabulary list (15 to 20 words) for your PowerPoint presentation. Your classmates will utilize this list during the Week 6 consecutive interpretation tasks.

Interpreting/Translation Technology

Having completed part one of this course, you should now have a basic understanding of *broadcast interpreting* and ways to improve your skills for practical application. Moving forward, in the next part of the course, you will:

- Build on your *consecutive interpreting (memory)* skills.
- Develop *consecutive interpreting (note-taking)* skills.
- Enhance your overall interpreting skills through *prosody* and *content shadowing*.
- Gain a grounding in *sight translation*.
- Practice *quick-response written vocabulary* tasks to both prepare you to consecutively interpret a presentation enhance your *note-taking* ability.

Warm-up 1
Consecutive Interpreting (Memory)

In this section of the course, you will practice ***consecutive interpreting (memory)*** using a series of Japanese stories by Kotaro Tanaka (1880-1941) (See Appendix C for a biography of this author). Each story features a shapeshifter, a well-known figure in Japanese folktales, and has been translated into English and specifically adapted (Appendix D) for this activity. Why stories?

1. **Logical Flow and Context:** Stories provide a natural flow, aiding in information retention.
2. **Rich Vocabulary and Idiomatic Expressions:** Challenge your linguistic skills.
3. **Engaging Narratives:** Capture attention, making details easier to remember.
4. **Diverse Scenarios:** Practice handling different types of content.
5. **Cultural Awareness:** Enhance your sensitivity to cultural elements.
6. **Real-Time Recall:** Mirrors actual interpreting scenarios, improving memory.
7. **Motivation:** Engaging nature makes practice more frequent and enjoyable.

The first story is called ***The Mystery of the Old Fox*** (Appendix D1). The story is divided into three parts, which your teacher will read aloud. Make sure that you know the meaning of the following challenging vocabulary/phrases before starting this activity.

- **Part 1**: Monk / Spiritual beliefs / Robes / Skull / Mimicking / Gestures / Blade of grass / Transformed
- **Part 2**: Processing / Horse neighing / Dismounted / Disguise

- **Part 3**: Chanting / Mantra / Wooden staff / Reveal / Fragments / Horrified / Nodded / Illusions / Buried / Deception

---

INSTRUCTIONS:

1. Close your book, listen carefully, and imagine the story as you hear it.
2. After each part, your teacher will pause, and you will need to retell the story in Japanese to a classmate.

INTERPRETING TIP 6 - *Use expressive voices*: Bring the characters to life by using different voices and expressions for each character. This helps listeners distinguish between characters and enhances their engagement with the story.

INTERPRETING TIP 7 - *Utilize vocal dynamics*: Vary your voice modulation to reflect different emotions, characters, and scenes in the story. Adjusting your pitch, volume, and pace can help create a more engaging and dynamic storytelling experience.

Warm-up 2
Shadowing

In the first part of the course, you practiced shadowing *British English* using **BBC Learning English**. To help you become skilled at understanding different accents, shadowing activities in the second part concentrate on *American English* available at **VOA (Voice of America) Learning English - Intermediate Level** website.

For this week's shadowing, follow these steps:

1. Use the provided QR code, below, to access the **VOA Learning English - Intermediate Level** website.
2. Select a program, listen and read along, imitate the rhythm and intonation.
3. Practice shadowing without the script until you can do it all.

VOA Learning English - Intermediate Level
https://learningenglish.voanews.com/p/5610.html

Task - Write the Japanese for the following:

1. CAT Tools: _______________________
2. Machine Translation: _______________________
3. Machine Interpreting: _______________________

Activity 1
Quick-response Vocabulary (Written)

Each of you created a three-minute presentation on *interpreting/translation technology* and put together a bilingual vocabulary list for the topics *CAT tools*, *machine translation*, and *machine interpreting*. Follow these instructions to improve your ability to quickly respond when interpreting a classmate's presentation on this topic:

1. Form groups of 2 to 4 members and exchange your bilingual vocabulary lists on *interpreting/translation technology* topics.
2. Take three minutes to memorize the Japanese and English words on the list given by your groupmate.
3. Your group member will read out English words for you to translate into Japanese and then Japanese words for you to translate into English in quick succession.
4. Repeat this activity for about 5 to 7 minutes to practice recalling and translating the vocabulary effectively.
5. Use the provided space, below, for this activity.

Activity 2
Consecutive Interpreting (Note-Taking)

This activity simulates real-world consecutive interpreting. You will use the presentations you have prepared about *interpreting/translation technology* to practice taking notes and accurately interpreting spoken content, focusing on capturing the speaker's message clearly and effectively, mirroring real-life challenges.

1. In your groups, play the three-minute English video presentations about *interpreting/translation technology* one by one.
2. The group member who practiced quick-response for the vocabulary used in the presentation will take notes while everyone else watches the presentation.
3. Using these notes, that member will then present the content in Japanese.
4. Use the provided space, below, for this activity. (Since this is your first time doing this activity, feel free to take notes in whatever manner suits you best; You will learn more about note-taking in future lessons.)
5. After listening to your groupmate's performance, use the provided evaluation table, below, to provide constructive feedback.

Evaluation Criteria	Rating (1-5)	Comments
Accuracy		Alignment with the original message
Clarity		Clarity of message delivery
Pronunciation		Pronunciation accuracy and clarity
Tone & Intonation		Matching speaker's tone and intonation
Pacing		Interpretation speed and flow
Confidence		Presenter's confidence and composure
Overall Performance		Overall interpretation evaluation

Preparation for Week 7

Task 1: Shadowing

Practice shadowing daily for 10-15 minutes, using materials like those on the **VOA Learning English - Intermediate Level** website. Consistent shadowing habits will enhance language fluency and pronunciation.

Task 2: 3-Minute English PowerPoint Presentation

Create a *3-minute* PowerPoint presentation in English about one or more of the following *interpreter training techniques*:

(1) *Prosody Shadowing* involves repeating speech while focusing on the prosodic features of the spoken language. It includes elements such as intonation, rhythm, stress, and pitch. The primary goal is to mimic the speaker's voice patterns, regardless of whether the meaning is fully understood. This practice helps develop a natural speaking style, improve their pronunciation, and better understand the tonal and rhythmic aspects of the language. The following are key features of *prosody shadowing*:

   i. **Intonation**: The rise and fall of the voice.
  ii. **Rhythm**: The pattern of sounds and silences in speech.
 iii. **Stress**: The emphasis placed on certain syllables or words.
  iv. **Pitch**: The highness or lowness of the voice.

(2) *Content Shadowing* focuses on accurately reproducing the actual content and meaning of the spoken language. In this technique, it is important to listen to the speech, comprehend it, and then immediately repeat it as accurately as possible. This practice emphasizes understanding and retaining the information, enhancing listening

comprehension and memory skills. The following are key features of *content shadowing:*

   i. **Comprehension**: Understanding the meaning of the speech.

  ii. **Accurate Reproduction**: Repeating the content faithfully.

 iii. **Immediate Recall**: Training memory and information retention.

(3) *Slash Reading* is a technique where a text is divided into manageable chunks or segments, often marked with slashes (/). This method aids interpreters by making complex sentences easier to digest and translate. By breaking down the text into smaller parts, interpreters can focus on rendering each segment accurately before moving on to the next. This approach helps build the ability to handle lengthy or intricate sentences and improves overall translation accuracy.

(4) *Sight Translation* involves reading a written text in one language and orally translating it into another language on the spot. It combines the skills of reading comprehension and oral interpretation, requiring quick mental processing and clear articulation. This practice is critical for interpreters as it enhances their ability to deliver accurate translations in real-time scenarios where written documents need to be conveyed promptly, such as in legal or medical settings.

Record and export your presentation in .mp4 format for file sharing with your classmates in Week 7.

Task 3: Short Bilingual Vocabulary List

Generate a bilingual (English and Japanese) key vocabulary list (15 to 20 words) for your PowerPoint presentation. Your classmates will utilize this list during the Week 7 consecutive interpretation tasks.

Interpreter Training Techniques

Warm-up 1
Consecutive Interpreting (Memory)

This week, you will listen to a story called ***The Fable of the Fox and Raccoon Dog*** (Appendix D2) in three parts. Your teacher will read each part. Make sure that you know the meaning of the following challenging vocabulary/phrases before starting this activity.

- **Part 1**: Raccoon dog / Talented / Governor / Curious / Transformed / Scholars / Guardian / Confidently / Wise / Hesitation
- **Part 2**: Disguised / Debate / Suspicious / Advisor / Wisdom / Proudly
- **Part 3**: Situation / Revealed / Sacred / Millennium

____

____

____

____

____

____

____

____

____

INSTRUCTIONS:

1. Close your book, listen carefully, and imagine the story as you hear it.
2. After each part, your teacher will pause, and you will need to retell the story in Japanese to your teammates.

INTERPRETING TIP 8 - *Pause for effect*: Utilize pauses strategically to build suspense, emphasize key points, or allow listeners to digest important information. Pause before a reveal to keep listeners on the edge of their seats.

INTERPRETING TIP 9 - *Movement and positioning*: Consider your positioning and movement in relation to the listeners. Moving around subtly or changing positions can maintain audience attention and create visual interest during the storytelling session.

Warm-up 2
Shadowing (Prosody and Content)

To help you become skilled at both *prosody* and *content shadowing*, this week you will shadow a presentation from **VOA (Voice of America) Learning English - Intermediate Level** twice: first using *prosody shadowing* and then using *content shadowing*.

- *Prosody Shadowing*: Focus on imitating the speaker's rhythm, intonation, and stress patterns.
- *Content Shadowing*: Focus on accurately reproducing the meaning and content of the speech.

For this week's shadowing practice, follow these steps:

1. Use the provided QR code below to access the **VOA Learning English - Intermediate Level** website.
2. Select a program, listen and read along, and imitate the rhythm and intonation (*Prosody Shadowing*).
3. Practice *prosody shadowing* without the script until you can shadow the entire presentation.
4. Return to the beginning of the presentation and practice *content shadowing*. After finishing, you should be able to explain the *content* of the program to a classmate.

VOA Learning English - Intermediate Level
https://learningenglish.voanews.com/p/5610.html

Warm-up 3
Slash Reading and Sight Translation

The following is a short talk about ***translation technology***. Before starting this activity, spend one minute scanning the talk for any words or vocabulary that you need to check the Japanese translation for. The underlined words are particularly challenging.

Slash Reading (One Minute):

1. As you read through the text, mark each significant pause or break with a slash (/).
2. Place slashes at points where you would naturally pause in speech, such as at commas, periods, or between phrases.

Sight Translation (Five Minutes):

1. Work in groups of two or three, taking turns to translate each paragraph from English to Japanese.
2. Focus on accurately conveying the meaning while maintaining a natural flow in your translations.
3. Take a moment to gather your thoughts before translating each segment, ensuring clarity and precision.
4. Encourage discussion and feedback within your group to improve translation skills and linguistic proficiency collaboratively.

ADVICE: If it takes one minute to read the original document, aim to sight translate (communicate) its meaning over three minutes. Why? Because spoken and written language are different. To keep your listeners engaged, deliver the information in shorter, easier-to-understand sentences.

One-minute Talk about Advances in Translation Technology

Hello, everyone!

Today, I'd like to briefly discuss the exciting advancements in translation technology. Over the past decade, we've witnessed significant changes driven by artificial intelligence and machine learning. Early translation tools, like simple word-for-word dictionaries, have evolved into sophisticated systems capable of understanding context and nuance.

One of the most impactful innovations is the development of **neural machine translation (NMT)**. Unlike traditional methods, which translated text in chunks, NMT considers entire sentences, making translations more accurate and fluent. Companies like Google and Microsoft have integrated NMT into their services, dramatically improving performance and reliability.

Moreover, **real-time translation** tools have become more accessible. Applications like Google Translate and Microsoft Translator now offer instant translation through voice and text, breaking down language barriers in everyday situations.

The use of translation technology in communication tools like email, messaging apps, and platforms like Zoom has transformed global business and collaboration by enabling multilingual communication.

As we continue to advance, the combination of AI, **big data**, and user feedback will only enhance these technologies, making translation more precise and accessible. The future of translation technology promises even greater innovations, ensuring that language is no longer a barrier to global understanding and collaboration.

Thank you!

Task - Write the Japanese for the following:

1. Prosody Shadowing: _______________________
2. Content Shadowing: _______________________
3. Slash Reading: _______________________
4. Sight Translation: _______________________

Activity 1
Quick-response Vocabulary (Written)

Each of you created a three-minute presentation on *interpreter training techniques* and put together a bilingual vocabulary list. In groups of 2 to 4, share and memorize bilingual vocabulary lists on *interpreter training techniques*. Spend 5 to 7 minutes taking turns translating English and Japanese words to practice memory recall and translation skills effectively.

____

____

____

____

____

____

____

____

____

____

____

____

____

____

____

Activity 2
Consecutive Interpreting (Note-taking)

This week, you will use the presentations you have prepared about *interpreter training techniques* to practice taking notes and accurately interpreting spoken content, focusing on capturing the speaker's message clearly and effectively, mirroring real-life challenges.

1. In your groups, play the three-minute English video presentations about *interpreter training techniques* one by one.
2. The member who practiced quick-response with the vocabulary for this presentation will take notes in the space provided while everyone else watches. They will then present in Japanese using these notes.
3. Be sure to take notes on each groupmate's performance for improvement, using the provided table.

____
____
____
____
____
____
____
____
____
____
____
____
____
____

Evaluation Criteria	Rating (1-5)	Comments
Accuracy		Alignment with the original message
Clarity		Clarity of message delivery
Pronunciation		Pronunciation accuracy and clarity
Tone & Intonation		Matching speaker's tone and intonation
Pacing		Interpretation speed and flow
Confidence		Presenter's confidence and composure
Overall Performance		Overall interpretation evaluation

Preparation for Week 8

Task 1: Shadowing

Practice prosody shadowing and content shadowing daily for 10-15 minutes, using materials like those on the **VOA Learning English - Intermediate Level** website. Consistent shadowing habits will enhance language fluency and pronunciation.

Task 2: 3-Minute English PowerPoint Presentation

Create a *3-minute* PowerPoint presentation in English about *note-taking techniques*. It's important to note that interpreters usually develop their own note-taking style, so the following are just ideas for your presentation.

(1) *Linear Notes*:

- Explanation: *Linear notes* mean jotting down info in the order it's spoken, creating a step-by-step record of what's said.
- Example: During interpreting, write down main points as they come up, like *Introduction → Topic A discussion → Conclusion*.

(2) *Symbol-based Notes*:

- Explanation: *Symbol-based notes* use simple symbols or abbreviations for faster note-taking.
- Example: Using symbols like **$** for *money*, **@** for *email*, or → for *leads to* helps capture important details efficiently.

(3) *Chunking*:

- Explanation: *Chunking* groups related info together for easier organization.
- Example: Grouping product features, prices, and feedback under separate headings helps in managing and remembering info.

(4) *Vertical Line Method*:

- Explanation: The *Vertical line method* divides notes into two columns for clear separation of source and target language notes.
- Example: By drawing a line down notes, keep English on the left and Japanese on the right for clear interpretation.

(5) *Selective Note-taking*:

- Explanation: *Selective note-taking* focuses on vital details to maintain concise and relevant notes.
- Example: Prioritize names, dates, and numbers over transcribing every word to accurately capture important details for effective interpretation.

Record and export your presentation in .mp4 format for file sharing with your classmates in Week 8.

Task 3: Short Bilingual Vocabulary List

Generate a bilingual (English and Japanese) key vocabulary list (15 to 20 words) for your PowerPoint presentation. Your classmates will utilize this list during the Week 8 consecutive interpretation tasks.

Note-taking Techniques

Warm-up 1
Consecutive Interpreting (Memory)

You will listen to a story called ***The Married Woman and Her Mysterious Housemate*** (Appendix D3) in three parts. Your teacher will read each part. Make sure that you know the meaning of the following challenging vocabulary/phrases before starting this activity.

- **Part 1**: Traveling salesman / Trembled / Corner
- **Part 2**: Melted / Exclaimed / Hugging
- **Part 3**: Interrupted / Intruder / Barged in / Chaos / Delicate / Lashed out / Club / Gripping / Transformed / Bewildered / Reeling / Passed away

---

INSTRUCTIONS:

1. Close your book, listen carefully, and imagine the story as you hear it.
2. After each part, your teacher will pause, and you will need to retell the story in Japanese to your teammates.

INTERPRETING TIP 10 - *Gesture and body language*: Use expressive gestures and body language to convey the characters' emotions and actions. Incorporating physical movements that align with the story can make the narration more lively and captivating for the listeners.

INTERPRETING TIP 11 - *Eye contact*: Maintain eye contact with your audience while storytelling to establish a connection and draw them into the narrative. Eye contact can help engage listeners and make them feel more involved in the storytelling experience.

Warm-up 2
Shadowing (Prosody and Content)

To improve your skills in *prosody* and ***content shadowing*** in preparation for simultaneous interpreting (Week 11 onward), you will shadow a **VOA Learning English - Intermediate Level** presentation twice this week. First, you will focus on mirroring the rhythm and intonation (***Prosody Shadowing***) <u>**while drawing a simple picture**</u>. Then, you will practice ***content shadowing***.

For this week's shadowing practice, follow these steps:

1. Use the QR code provided to access the **VOA Learning English - Intermediate Level** site.
2. Choose a program, listen, read along, and imitate the rhythm and intonation (***Prosody Shadowing***).
3. While practicing ***prosody shadowing***, <u>**draw a simple picture or an animated character**</u> you like on a piece of paper.
4. Practice prosody shadowing without the script until you can shadow the entire presentation.
5. Start over from the beginning of the presentation and practice ***content shadowing***.

VOA Learning English - Intermediate Level
https://learningenglish.voanews.com/p/5610.html

Warm-up 3
Slash Reading and Sight Translation

The following is a short talk about the effectiveness of ***prosody*** and ***content shadowing***. Before starting this activity, spend one minute scanning the talk for any words or vocabulary that you need to check the Japanese translation for.

Slash Reading (One Minute):

- As you read the text, mark each significant pause or break with a slash (/) at points like commas, periods, or between phrases where you would naturally pause in speech.

Sight Translation (Five Minutes):

- In groups of two to three, take turns translating paragraphs from English to Japanese, emphasizing clear meaning and smooth flow.
- Pause before each translation for clarity.
- Discuss and give feedback in your group to enhance translation skills and language proficiency together.

One-minute Talk about the Effectiveness of Prosody and Content Shadowing

Hello, everyone!

Today, I want to delve into the effectiveness of *prosody* and *content shadowing*, essential techniques in language learning and interpreting skills. Through *prosody shadowing*, by mirroring the speaker's rhythm, stress, and intonation, and *content shadowing*, accurately reproducing meaning and content, language learners and interpreters refine their ability to convey messages precisely and fluently.

Moreover, incorporating activities like drawing a picture or scribbling while practicing *prosody* and *content shadowing* not only enhances focus but also stimulates cognitive functions. These creative tasks aid in improving concentration and fostering multitasking abilities, crucial skills in preparation for simultaneous interpreting scenarios.

While technological advancements have transformed translation, the human touch provided by prosody and content shadowing infuses interpretation with depth and nuance. These traditional techniques, when integrated with modern tools, not only enhance understanding and communication but also elevate the artistic aspects of interpretation.

By harmonizing human interpretation skills with technological progress, we can effectively bridge language barriers, nurturing global cooperation and mutual comprehension. The future holds exciting prospects where this blend of traditional and modern approaches will continue to unite people across the globe.

Thank you!

Activity 1
Quick-response Vocabulary (Written)

Each of you created a three-minute presentation on ***note-taking techniques*** and put together a bilingual vocabulary list. In groups of 2 to 4, share and memorize bilingual vocabulary lists on interpreter training techniques. Spend 5 to 7 minutes taking turns translating English and Japanese words to practice memory recall and translation skills effectively.

Activity 2
Consecutive Interpreting (Note-taking)

This week, you will use the presentations you have prepared about ***note-taking techniques*** to practice taking notes and accurately interpreting spoken content, focusing on capturing the speaker's message clearly and effectively, mirroring real-life challenges.

1. In your groups, play the three-minute English video presentations about ***note-taking techniques*** one by one.
2. The member who practiced quick-response with the vocabulary for this presentation will take notes in the space provided while everyone else watches. They will then present in Japanese using these notes.
3. Be sure to take notes on each classmate's performance for improvement, using the provided table.

Evaluation Criteria	Rating (1-5)	Comments
Accuracy		Alignment with the original message
Clarity		Clarity of message delivery
Pronunciation		Pronunciation accuracy and clarity
Tone & Intonation		Matching speaker's tone and intonation
Pacing		Interpretation speed and flow
Confidence		Presenter's confidence and composure
Overall Performance		Overall interpretation evaluation

Preparation for Week 9

Task 1: Shadowing

Practice prosody shadowing and content shadowing daily for 10-15 minutes, using materials like those on the **VOA Learning English - Intermediate Level** website. Consistent shadowing habits will enhance language fluency and pronunciation.

Task 2: 3-Minute English PowerPoint Presentation

Create a **_3-minute_** PowerPoint presentation in English about **_companies/organizations that recruit interpreters_**. Include details such as:

- **_Job Responsibilities_** (e.g., interpreting tasks and duties);
- Required **_Knowledge and Skills_** (e.g., proficiency in consecutive and whispered interpreting, business expertise);
- **_Qualifications_** (e.g., TOEIC 800+, EIKEN Pre-1, Bachelor's degree in English, Bookkeeping certification - level 3);
- **_Compensation_** ($$).

The following sites contain information that you may find useful:

Japan Translators Federation	Medical Interpreting Association of Japan
https://www.jtf.jp/	https://www.gi-miaj.org/

Japan Association of Conference Interpreters	Japan Association of Translators
 https://www.japan-interpreters.org/	https://jat.org/

Record and export your presentation in .mp4 format for file sharing with your classmates in Week 9.

Task 3: Short Bilingual Vocabulary List

Generate a bilingual (English and Japanese) key vocabulary list (15 to 20 words) for your PowerPoint presentation. Your classmates will utilize this list during the Week 9 consecutive interpretation tasks.

Interpreter Recruitment

Warm-up 1
Consecutive Interpreting (Memory)

You will listen to a story called ***The Raccoon Dog and the Haiku Poet*** (Appendix D4) in three parts. Your teacher will read each part. Make sure that you know the meaning of the following challenging vocabulary/phrases before starting this activity.

- **Part 1:** Persimmons / Ise Grand Shrine / Poetic talents / Stand out / Serene / Wondered / Crisp air / Companionship / Newfound warmth
- **Part 2:** Routine / Shared comfort / Whispered / Plea / Safeguard / Farewell / Passed away / Mysterious / Amidst / Nods / Honor / Bond
- **Part 3:** Circulate / Cherished / Legends / Harmony / Loyal / Sparking curiosity / Mysterious / Embraced / Deep respect / Interconnectedness Living beings / Generations / Enduring / Thrived / Profound appreciation / Tranquility / Inspire

____

____

____

____

____

____

____

____

____

____

INSTRUCTIONS:

1. Close your book, listen carefully, and imagine the story as you hear it.
2. After each part, your teacher will pause, and you will need to retell the story in Japanese to your teammates.

INTERPRETING TIP 12- *Facial expressions*: Use facial expressions to convey emotions and reactions as you narrate the story. Expressive facial cues can add depth to the characters and help convey the mood of the story effectively.

Warm-up 2
Shadowing (Prosody and Content)

This week, you will practice *prosody* and *content shadowing* for better simultaneous interpreting skills. You will shadow a **VOA Learning English - Intermediate Level** presentation twice. First, focus on mimicking the rhythm and intonation (*Prosody Shadowing*) while doing simple arithmetic. Then, practice *content shadowing*.

For this week's shadowing practice, follow these steps:

1. Use the QR code provided to access the **VOA Learning English - Intermediate Level** site.
2. Choose a program, listen, read along, and imitate the rhythm and intonation (*Prosody Shadowing*).
3. While practicing *prosody shadowing*, do the ten <u>simple arithmetic</u> questions on the next page.
4. Start over from the beginning of the presentation and practice *content shadowing*.

VOA Learning English - Intermediate Level
https://learningenglish.voanews.com/p/5610.html

Ten Arithmetic Questions

(1) What is 25 + 13?	(6) Add 3.5 and 6.25.
(2) Subtract 48 from 92.	(7) Find the product of 12 and 11.
(3) Multiply 7 by 9.	(8) Subtract 63 from 108.
(4) Divide 56 by 8.	(9) Divide 84 by 7.
(5) Calculate 4 squared.	(10) What is 15% of 200?

Warm-up 3
Slash Reading and Sight Translation

The following is a short talk about a heroic Japanese interpreter called **Chiune Sugihara**. Before starting this activity, spend one minute scanning the talk for any words or vocabulary that you need to check the Japanese translation for.

Slash Reading (One Minute):

- As you read the text, mark each significant pause or break with a slash (/) at points like commas, periods, or between phrases where you would naturally pause in speech.

Sight Translation (Five Minutes):

- In groups of two to three, take turns translating paragraphs from English to Japanese, emphasizing clear meaning and smooth flow.
- Pause before each translation for clarity.
- Discuss and give feedback in your group to enhance translation skills and language proficiency together.

One-minute Talk about Chiune Sugihara:
The Heroic Interpreter

Hello, everyone!

Today, I want to share the inspiring story of Chiune Sugihara, a Japanese diplomat and interpreter during World War II, whose courageous actions saved thousands of lives. Sugihara, stationed in Lithuania, was fluent in multiple languages and used his skills in a profound way.

As Jews fled from Nazi-occupied Poland, they desperately needed visas to escape. Despite strict instructions from his government, Sugihara chose to issue transit visas against orders, recognizing the life-or-death situation these refugees faced. Over roughly four weeks in 1940, he worked tirelessly, often for long hours each day, hand-writing over 2,000 visas. Each visa represented not just an individual but often whole families, ultimately saving around 6,000 lives.

Sugihara continued his lifesaving work even until the day he left the consulate, throwing visas out the train window. Later reprimanded by his government, Sugihara's quiet heroism remained largely unknown until decades later, when he was finally honored as one of the Righteous Among the Nations.

Chiune Sugihara's story is a powerful example of how interpreters and diplomats can make a significant impact through their moral courage and dedication. His legacy reminds us that our skills and positions can be used for tremendous good, even in the face of great challenges.

Thank you!

Activity 1
Quick-response Vocabulary (Written)

Each of you created a three-minute presentation on ***companies/organizations recruiting interpreters*** and put together a bilingual vocabulary list. In groups of 2 to 4, share and memorize bilingual vocabulary lists on interpreter training techniques. Spend 5 to 7 minutes taking turns translating English and Japanese words to practice memory recall and translation skills effectively.

Activity 2
Consecutive Interpreting (Note-taking)

This week, you will use the presentations you have prepared about ***companies/organizations recruiting interpreters*** to practice taking notes and accurately interpreting spoken content, focusing on capturing the speaker's message clearly and effectively, mirroring real-life challenges.

1. In your groups, play the three-minute English video presentations about ***companies/organizations recruiting interpreters*** one by one.
2. The member who practiced quick-response with the vocabulary for this presentation will take notes in the space provided while everyone else watches. They will then present in Japanese using these notes.
3. Be sure to take notes on each classmate's performance for improvement, using the provided table.

Evaluation Criteria	Rating (1-5)	Comments
Accuracy		Alignment with the original message
Clarity		Clarity of message delivery
Pronunciation		Pronunciation accuracy and clarity
Tone & Intonation		Matching speaker's tone and intonation
Pacing		Interpretation speed and flow
Confidence		Presenter's confidence and composure
Overall Performance		Overall interpretation evaluation

Preparation for Week 10

Task 1: Shadowing

Practice prosody shadowing and content shadowing daily for 10-15 minutes, using materials like those on the **VOA Learning English - Intermediate Level** website. Consistent shadowing habits will enhance language fluency and pronunciation.

Task 2: Review

Review what you have learned over the past four weeks.

Consecutive Interpreting Review

Summary of Learning

Welcome to the second review lesson. Over the past four weeks, you have developed your interpreting skills in several key areas:

(1) *Consecutive Interpreting (Memory)* - You have practiced interpreting four three-part stories and learned how to deliver interpretations in an engaging manner.

(2) *Prosody* and *Content Shadowing* - You have learned about the difference between *prosody* and *content shadowing* and practiced *prosody shadowing* while focusing on a secondary task in preparation for *simultaneous interpreting*.

(3) *Slash Reading* and *Sight Translation* - You have used *slash reading* techniques to break down one-minute talks on the following topics into manageable chunks to facilitate smoother and more accurate *sight translations*:

- Advances in translation technology
- The effectiveness of prosody and content shadowing
- The story of Japanese linguist Chiune Sugihara

(4) ***Knowledge about the Field of Interpreting*** - You have deepened your understanding about field of interpreting through presentations on:

- Interpreting/translation technology
- Interpreter training techniques
- Interpreter note-taking
- Companies/organizations hiring interpreters

(5) ***Quick Response Written Vocabulary*** Activities - You have engaged in four ***quick-response vocabulary writing*** activities to enhance your ***consecutive interpreting note-taking*** ability.

(6) ***Consecutive Interpreting (Note-taking)*** - You have practiced ***consecutive interpreting*** presentations about the field of interpreting with a focus on effective ***note-taking***.

This review lesson will focus is on:

- Reviewing and assessing the effectiveness of what you've learned.
- Engaging in a short ***consecutive interpreting (note-taking)*** test in front of your classmates to showcase your progress.

Learning Comprehension Check

(You can find the answers to these questions in the sight translation readings. Write your answers in English or Japanese.)

(1) What has driven significant changes in translation technology over the past decade?

____

____

____

(2) What makes neural machine translation (NMT) more effective than traditional translation methods?

____

____

____

(3) How have real-time translation tools impacted global business and collaboration?

____

____

____

(4) What are the two techniques discussed in the talk that are essential for language learning and interpreting skills?

____

____

____

(5) How do activities like drawing or scribbling while practicing shadowing benefit interpreters?

____

____

____

(6) How do prosody and content shadowing complement technological advancements in translation?

____

____

____

(7) What actions did Chiune Sugihara take during World War II that saved thousands of lives?

____

____

____

(8) How many visas did Chiune Sugihara hand-write over the span of approximately four weeks in 1940?

____

____

(9) When did Chiune Sugihara receive recognition for his actions, and what honor was he given?

____

____

____

Consecutive Interpreting Delivery Review

In this part of the course, you have learned an additional *seven interpreting tips* to enhance your *consecutive interpreting delivery*. Use the space below to describe each tip in *Japanese*. Explain which you found to be the most effective and why.

Shadowing Review

Over the past four weeks, you have done four *prosody* and *content shadowing* exercises with segments from **Voice Of America**. Use the space on the following page to answer the following questions in English or Japanese:

(1) How have these shadowing activities improved your ability to shadow accurately?

(2) How often have you practiced shadowing outside of class?

(3) What materials have you used for practicing shadowing outside of class?

(4) What steps can you take to further improve your shadowing technique?

____
____
____
____
____
____
____

Slash Reading and Sight Translation Review

Starting in Week 7, you completed three *slash reading* and *sight translation* tasks. Write your answers to the following questions (in Japanese or English) in the space provided below.

(1) *Sight Translation Situations*: In what situations do you think interpreters need to use their sight translation skills?

(2) *Strengths and Weaknesses*: What are your strengths and weaknesses with sight translation?

(3) *Preparation Time*: How long did it take you to prepare for sight translating the one-minute talks in this part of the course?

____
____
____
____
____
____
____
____
____

Consecutive Interpreting Assessment Review

Your classmates have provided feedback on your *consecutive interpreting (note-taking)* in the following areas: *accuracy, clarity, pronunciation, tone & intonation, pacing, confidence*, and *overall performance*. Reflect on your progress and the feedback you have received to answer the following questions in English or Japanese:

(1) What do you consider to be your *consecutive interpreting strengths and weaknesses*?

(2) How do you intend to *enhance your consecutive interpreting* performance from now on?

Consecutive Interpreting Test
(Note-taking)

Part 1: 15-Minute Quick-Response Vocabulary Warm-up

Your teacher will assign you a test partner. Exchange your bilingual vocabulary lists for one of the following presentations (Choose the presentation you performed best on):

- Interpreting/translation technology
- Interpreter training techniques
- Interpreter note-taking
- Companies/organizations recruiting interpreters

You have fifteen minutes to review and remember the vocabulary. Use the space provided below to practice *quick-response vocabulary (writing)* with your test partner.

Part 2: Consecutive Interpreting Performance

The mp4 presentations you selected will be played to the class. When your test partner's English presentation is played, take notes. Once it has finished, use your notes to provide a Japanese consecutive interpretation to the class. After you finish, evaluate your performance for improvement using the evaluation table, below.

ADVICE: Make sure to apply the techniques you've learned about consecutive interpreting to ensure your interpretation is engaging.

Evaluation Criteria	Rating (1-5)	Comments
Accuracy		Alignment with the original message
Clarity		Clarity of message delivery
Pronunciation		Pronunciation accuracy and clarity
Tone & Intonation		Matching speaker's tone and intonation
Pacing		Interpretation speed and flow
Confidence		Presenter's confidence and composure
Overall Performance		Overall interpretation evaluation

Preparation for Week 11

Task 1: Prosody and Content Shadowing

Practice shadowing daily for 10-15 minutes, using materials like those on the **BBC Learning English** website or **Voice Of America** website. Consistent shadowing habits will not only enhance language fluency and pronunciation but also prepare you for simultaneous interpreting.

Task 2: 3-Minute English PowerPoint Presentation

Prepare a *3-minute* English PowerPoint presentation about *companies/organizations recruiting English language specialists*. Include details such as:

- *Job Responsibilities* (e.g., language related tasks and duties);
- Required *Knowledge and Skills*;
- *Qualifications* (e.g., TOEIC 800+, EIKEN Pre-1, Bachelor's degree in English, Bookkeeping certification - level 3);
- *Compensation* ($$).

The two following links should give you some ideas:

19 Jobs that Require English	36 English Speaking Jobs
https://ten-navi.com/hacks/article-83-14562	https://tenshoku-web.jp/english-speaking-jobs/

Record and export your presentation in .mp4 format for file sharing with your classmates in Week 11.

Task 3: Short Bilingual Vocabulary List

Generate a bilingual key vocabulary list (English and Japanese) for your PowerPoint presentation. Your classmates will utilize this list in preparation for Week 11 simultaneous interpretating tasks.

English Language Specialist Recruitment

You have completed sections 1 and 2 of this course, where the focus was on honing your *broadcast interpreting* and *consecutive interpreting* skills. In the final part of this course, you will progress onto *simultaneous interpreting*. To build on your previous learning, the upcoming part will involve:

- Practicing *consecutive interpreting (note-taking)* using Kotaro Tanaka's stories translated and adapted into English, with a provided vocabulary list to enhance your understanding and lexicon.
- *Shadowing* to refine *prosody* and *content* comprehension while taking notes using a bilingual podcast.
- Learning effective audience engagement techniques for *sight translation*.
- Transitioning from *written* to *verbal/spoken quick-response vocabulary* tasks.
- *Simultaneously interpreting* classmates' presentations on interpreting-related topics.

Warm-up 1
Consecutive Interpreting (Note-taking)

Listen to your teacher read a story called ***Mujina: The Mischievous Shape-Shifter of Kiinokuni Hill*** (Appendix D5) in three parts. Make sure that you know the meaning of the following challenging vocabulary/phrases before starting this activity.

- **Part 1**: Respected merchant / Moat / Eerie / Sob / Empathy / Curiosity / Spine / Gasping
- **Part 2**: Refuge / Sought comfort / Elderly / Featureless / Simmering / Broth / Spirits / Roaming / Sorrow
- **Part 3**: Maidens / Ghostly beings / Weaving fear / Shivered / Legend / Etched in their minds / Mortals / Spirit realm

INSTRUCTIONS:

1. Listen attentively as your teacher reads each part of the story.
2. Visualize the story in your mind as you hear it and take notes to help remember the key points.
3. After each part, your teacher will pause. Use your notes to retell the story in Japanese to one of your classmates.

Warm-up 2
Shadowing (Prosody and Content)

In this final part of the course, you will practice *prosody* and *content shadowing* using a bilingual (English and Japanese) podcast) called **Bilingual News**. For this week's shadowing practice, follow these steps:

1. Use the QR code provided to access the latest bilingual talk on the **Bilingual News** website.
2. When the presenters speak English, *prosody shadow in English*; when they speak in Japanese, *prosody shadow in Japanese*. Do this for 5 minutes.
3. While practicing *prosody shadowing*, do the ten <u>simple arithmetic</u> questions on the next page.
4. Start over from the beginning of the presentation and practice *content shadowing*.
5. While practicing *content shadowing*, take notes about what the presenters are saying.

Bilingual News
https://bilingualnews.jp/podcastpage/

Ten Arithmetic Questions

(1) What is 38 + 21?	(6) Add 8.7 and 4.3.
(2) Subtract 24 from 59.	(7) Find the product of 13 and 19.
(3) Multiply 6 by 5.	(8) Subtract 53 from 96.
(4) Divide 54 by 6.	(9) Divide 45 by 5.
(5) Calculate 12 squared.	(10) What is 18% of 180?

Warm-up 3
Slash Reading and Sight Translation

The following is a short talk about *when and where interpreters use sight translation*. Before you start, double-check any words you need to confirm the Japanese translations for.

Slash Reading (One Minute):

- As you read the text, mark each significant pause or break with a slash (/) at points like commas, periods, or between phrases where you would naturally pause in speech.

Sight Translation (Five Minutes):

- In groups of two to three, take turns translating paragraphs from English to Japanese, emphasizing clear meaning and smooth flow.

Presentation Tips:

(1) *Identify and prioritize the main ideas or key points* to ensure clear and concise translation.
(2) *Maintain good eye contact* with the group to establish a connection and convey confidence.
(3) *Use hand gestures purposefully* to emphasize key points and enhance understanding.

One-minute Talk
about When and Where Interpreters
Use Sight Translation

Hello, everyone!

Today, I'll be talking about how interpreters use *sight translation* to communicate vital information in a multitude of settings. At conferences and meetings, they adeptly translate documents and presentations to ensure seamless discussions. In legal contexts, interpreters are essential for sight translating legal documents like contracts and reports during court proceedings and meetings with attorneys.

In medical settings, interpreters play a crucial role in translating medical records, prescriptions, and consent forms for patients during appointments. Within educational environments, interpreters assist students with limited language proficiency by sight translating instructions, tests, and educational materials.

During business negotiations, interpreters facilitate understanding by translating contracts, emails, and other key documents between international partners. Moreover, at public events, interpreters enable effective communication by translating speeches, announcements, and written content for diverse audiences.

These examples underscore the significance of *sight translation* in fostering clarity and effective communication across a range of sectors.

Thank you.

Activity 1
Quick-response Vocabulary (Spoken)

In Part 2 of this course, you practiced *written quick-response vocabulary* activities for better *note-taking* during *consecutive interpreting*. Now, in preparation for *simultaneous interpreting*, you'll do a similar activity, but instead of writing the words, say *them out loud*. Here's how:

1. Your group member will read English words for you to say Japanese, then Japanese words for you say English, one after another.
2. Practice this for 5 to 7 minutes to improve your recall and speed.

Activity 2
Simultaneous Interpreting (Note-taking)

This activity simulates real-world simultaneous interpreting. You will use the presentations you have prepared about *companies/organizations recruiting English language specialists* to practice, focusing on capturing the speaker's message clearly and effectively.

1. In your groups, play the three-minute video presentations about *companies/organizations recruiting English language specialists* one by one.
2. The group member who practiced quick-response vocabulary will listen to the presentation with headphones and *simultaneously interpret* it aloud while everyone else watches.
3. If you have trouble while interpreting, quickly note down relevant words/phrases in the space below and provide a consecutive interpretation after the presentation.
4. Use the provided table to evaluate both your own and your group members' performance for improvement.

____

____

____

____

____

____

____

____

____

____

Evaluation Criteria	Rating (1-5)	Comments
Accuracy		Alignment with the original message
Clarity		Clarity of message delivery
Pronunciation		Pronunciation accuracy and clarity
Tone & Intonation		Matching speaker's tone and intonation
Pacing		Interpretation speed and flow
Confidence		Presenter's confidence and composure
Overall Performance		Overall interpretation evaluation

Preparation for Week 12

Task 1: Shadowing

Practice shadowing daily for 10-15 minutes, using materials like those on the **Bilingual News** website. Consistent shadowing habits will enhance language fluency and pronunciation.

Task 2: 3-Minute English PowerPoint Presentation

Prepare a 3-minute English presentation about *interpreter qualifications and standards*. Describe each qualification in terms of:

- Interpreter Skills and Sub-skills
- Interpreter Knowledge
- Domain Knowledge
- Situational Knowledge

Ref. *Interpreter Skills/Knowledge* (Appendix E).

The following are links to qualifications in Japan and the UK:

JNTO Guide Interpreter Examination	CIOL Qualifications (UK)
https://www.jnto.go.jp/projects/visitor-support/interpreter-guide-exams/	https://www.ciol.org.uk/ciol-qualifications

The following are links to internationally recognized standards:

ISO in Japanese	ISO Interpreting Services Recommendations
https://www.infosta.or.jp/iso/tc37/about-TC37-SC5.html	https://www.iso.org/standard/63544.html
ISO Simultaneous Interpreting Requirements	**ISO Legal Interpreting Requirements**
https://www.iso.org/obp/ui/#iso:std:iso:20108:ed-1:v1:en	https://www.iso.org/standard/67327.html

Record and export your presentation in .mp4 format for file sharing with your classmates in Week 12.

Task 3: Short Bilingual Vocabulary List

Generate a bilingual key vocabulary list (English and Japanese) for your PowerPoint presentation. Your classmates will utilize this list to prepare for Week 12 simultaneous interpretation tasks.

Interpreter Qualifications/ Standards

Warm-up 1
Consecutive Interpreting (Note-taking)

Listen to your teacher read the *first episode* of a story called *Secrets of the Fox's Ledger* (Appendix D6.1) in three parts. Check the meaning of the following vocabulary/phrases before starting.

- **Part 1**: Serene / Wandering merchant / Household manager / Crisp night air / Slumber / Presence / Stirred / Looming / Figure / Startled / Exclaimed / Instant / Mysterious / Fleeting smile / Swiftly / Vanishing / Bewildered / Recounted / Eerie encounter / Vanished into thin air / Meticulously / Trace / Intruder / Night wore on / Shrouding / Veil of mystery
- **Part 2**: Soft hues of dawn / Lingered / Casting a shadow / Demeanor / Weight of uncertainty / Alert / Trio / Vigilance / Ajar / Dim light / Restless / Wary / Muttered / Jolted / Prompting / Elusive presence / Puzzled / Apprehensive
- **Part 3**: Words carried a weight of unknown intent / Permitted / Hearts racing / Enigma / Echoed / Consumed by thoughts / Inexplicable / First light of dawn / Trepidation /Curiosity

---

INSTRUCTIONS:

1. Listen attentively as your teacher reads each part of the story.
2. Visualize the story in your mind as you hear it and take notes to help you remember the key points.
3. After each part, your teacher will pause. Use your notes to retell the story in Japanese to one of your classmates.

Warm-up 2
Shadowing (Prosody and Content)

Practice *prosody* and *content shadowing* using **Bilingual News**.

1. Use the QR code provided to access the latest bilingual talk on the **Bilingual News** website.
2. When the presenters speak English, *prosody shadow in English*; when they speak in Japanese, *prosody shadow in Japanese* (5 minutes). While doing this, solve the ten <u>simple arithmetic</u> questions on the next page.
3. Start over from the beginning of the presentation and practice *content shadowing*, taking notes in the space below the arithmetic questions on what the presenters are saying.

Bilingual News
https://bilingualnews.jp/podcastpage/

Ten Arithmetic Questions

(1) What is 34 + 19?	(6) Add 7.3 and 8.65.
(2) Subtract 52 from 105.	(7) Find the product of 14 and 12.
(3) Multiply 8 by 6.	(8) Subtract 74 from 137.
(4) Divide 72 by 9.	(9) Divide 90 by 5.
(5) Calculate 5 squared.	(10) What is 20% of 150?

Warm-up 3
Slash Reading and Sight Translation

The following is a short talk about *interpreter qualifications*. Before you start, double-check any words you need to confirm the Japanese translations for.

Slash Reading (One Minute):

- As you read the text, mark each significant pause or break with a slash (/) at points like commas, periods, or between phrases where you would naturally pause in speech.

Sight Translation (Five Minutes):

- In groups of two to three, take turns translating paragraphs from English to Japanese, emphasizing clear meaning and smooth flow.

Presentation Tips:

(4) Make sure that you *grasp the context* of the text to convey the intended meaning effectively.

(5) Ensure your *posture is upright and open* to project professionalism and engagement.

(6) Be *mindful of your body movements* to avoid distractions and maintain focus on the translation.

One-minute Talk
about Interpreter Qualifications

Hello, everyone!

Official *interpreter qualifications* are integral to upholding professionalism and precision in interpretation globally. For conference interpreters navigating diplomatic realms, certifications from organizations like AIIC set high standards worldwide.

In legal and government sectors, certifications are vital. In the UK, the CIOL (Chartered Institute of Linguists) offers certifications, ensuring quality interpretation in legal settings internationally.

Healthcare interpreters, seeking certifications from bodies like CCHI and NBCMI in the US or NAATI (National Accreditation Authority for Translators and Interpreters) in Australia, provide critical language support in medical contexts.

For community interpreters in Australia, certifications from organizations like NAATI boost language services in diverse communities, promoting effective communication.

International organizations like the United Nations recruit skilled interpreters through the UN Language Competitive Exam for diplomatic roles globally, ensuring consistent and high-quality interpretation services.

Educational qualifications, language proficiency, and practical experience are shared prerequisites across interpreter certifications worldwide, fostering excellence and ethical standards in the interpreting profession.

Thank you!

Activity 1
Quick-response Vocabulary (Spoken)

To *prepare to simultaneously interpret* a groupmate's presentation about *interpreter qualifications and standards*, give your bilingual vocabulary list to your partner who will interpret your presentation. Spend five minutes reviewing the words in both languages, and then practice *quick-response vocabulary*. Here's how:

1. Your group member will read English words for you to say Japanese, then Japanese words for you say English, one after another.
2. Practice this for 5 to 7 minutes to improve your recall and speed.

Activity 2
Simultaneous Interpreting (Note-taking)

This activity simulates real-world simultaneous interpreting. You will use the presentations you have prepared about *interpreter qualifications and standards* to practice, focusing on capturing the speaker's message clearly and effectively.

1. In your groups, play the three-minute video presentations about *interpreter qualifications and standards* one by one.
2. The group member who practiced quick-response vocabulary will listen to the presentation with headphones and *simultaneously interpret* it aloud while everyone else watches.
3. If you have trouble while interpreting, quickly note down relevant words/phrases in the space below and provide a consecutive interpretation after the presentation.
4. Use the provided table to evaluate both your own and your group members' performance for improvement.

Evaluation Criteria	Rating (1-5)	Comments
Accuracy		Alignment with the original message
Clarity		Clarity of message delivery
Pronunciation		Pronunciation accuracy and clarity
Tone & Intonation		Matching speaker's tone and intonation
Pacing		Interpretation speed and flow
Confidence		Presenter's confidence and composure
Overall Performance		Overall interpretation evaluation

Preparation for Week 13

Task 1: Shadowing

Practice shadowing daily for 10-15 minutes, using materials like those on the **Bilingual News** website. Consistent shadowing habits will enhance language fluency and pronunciation.

Task 2: 3-Minute English PowerPoint Presentation

Prepare a 3-minute English presentation about *professional and academic interpreter associations*. Summarize the activities of one or more *professional association* and one or more *academic association*.

Professional Associations primarily aim to support interpreters in their work. For example, they may:

1. Provide information about training programs and qualifications for interpreters.
2. Host events where interpreters can exchange ideas and improve their skills.
3. Offer information about interpreting job opportunities.
4. Maintain a database of interpreter agencies:
    - Clients can search these databases when they need an interpreter.
    - Interpreters can search these databases when they are looking for employment.
5. Maintain a database of interpreters for employers to find and hire interpreters.
6. Protect and defend interpreters from dishonest employers.
7. Protect and defend interpreting clients from dishonest employers and unqualified interpreters.

Professional Associations

JACI: Japan Association of Conference Interpreters	JAT: Japan Association of Translators
 https://www.japan-interpreters.org/	 https://jat.org/
JTF: Japan Translation Federation	General Incorporated Medical Interpreting Association of Japan
 https://www.jtf.jp/	 http://gi-miaj.org/
Japan Guide Association	Hiroshima Interpreter and Guide Association
 https://www.jga21c.or.jp/	https://j-higa.net/

Academic Associations primarily aim to enhance knowledge about interpreting. For example, they may:

1. Host events where interpreting researchers can present their findings on:
    - Interpreter training programs
    - The working conditions of interpreters
    - The latest interpreter technology
    - Interpreter qualifications
    - The quality of interpreting
    - Interpreting standards (e.g., ISO)
2. Publish journals featuring the latest research from interpreting scholars.
3. Assist in creating new professional associations for niche interpreter specializations. For instance, if there is no association for ***sports interpreters***, researchers may collaborate to establish one.

Academic Associations

JAITS: Japan Association for Interpreting and Translation Studies	APTIS: The Association of Programmes in Translation and Interpreting Studies

https://jaits.jpn.org/home/index.html	https://www.aptis-translation-interpreting.org/

Record and export your presentation in .mp4 format for file sharing with your classmates in Week 13.

Task 3: Short Bilingual Vocabulary List

Generate a bilingual key vocabulary list (English and Japanese) for your PowerPoint presentation. Your classmates will utilize this list to prepare for Week 13 simultaneous interpretation tasks.

Professional and Academic Interpreter Associations

Warm-up 1
Consecutive Interpreting (Note-taking)

Listen to your teacher read the *second episode* of *Secret's of the Fox's Ledger* (Appendix D6.2) in three parts. Check the meaning of the following vocabulary/phrases before starting.

- **Part 4:** Cautiously / Lost in thought / Folded arms / Awakened / Scowled / Disturbing / Unfazed / Annoyed / Dismissed / Bothering / Sequestered / Distant behavior / Erratic behavior / Puzzled
- **Part 5:** Seclusion / Signaling / Ominous / Presence / Lurking / Discerned / Unsettling / Malevolent force / Confiding / Deep in thought / Contemplated / Mysterious / Entity / Pondering / Foreboding / Enveloped / Vigilant / Anticipating / Haunting / Anomalies / Under the cover of darkness / Revelation
- **Part 6:** Dagger / Lunged / Sinking / Distress / Reverberated / Peering / Anticipated / Sinister / Hushed tone / Glimmer of familiarity / Manifestation / Seeking solace

INSTRUCTIONS:

1. Listen attentively as your teacher reads each part of the story.
2. Visualize the story in your mind as you hear it and take notes to help you remember the key points.
3. After each part, your teacher will pause. Use your notes to retell the story in Japanese to one of your classmates.

Warm-up 2
Shadowing (Prosody and Content)

Practice *prosody* and *content shadowing* using **Bilingual News.**

1. Use the QR code provided to access the latest bilingual talk on the **Bilingual News** website.
2. When the presenters speak English, *prosody shadow in English*; when they speak in Japanese, *prosody shadow in Japanese* (5 minutes). While doing this, solve the ten <u>simple arithmetic</u> questions on the next page.
3. Start over from the beginning of the presentation and practice *content shadowing*, taking notes in the space below the arithmetic questions on what the presenters are saying.

Bilingual News
https://bilingualnews.jp/podcastpage/

Ten Arithmetic Questions

(1) What is 47 + 16?	(6) Add 4.5 and 5.75.
(2) Subtract 36 from 89.	(7) Find the product of 10 and 15.
(3) Multiply 5 by 8.	(8) Subtract 45 from 120.
(4) Divide 64 by 8.	(9) Divide 72 by 8.
(5) Calculate 6 squared.	(10) What is 25% of 160?

Warm-up 3
Slash Reading and Sight Translation

The following is a short talk about *international interpreter associations*. Before you start, double-check any words you need to confirm the Japanese translations for.

Slash Reading (One Minute):

- As you read the text, mark each significant pause or break with a slash (/) at points like commas, periods, or between phrases where you would naturally pause in speech.

Sight Translation (Five Minutes):

- In groups of two to three, take turns translating paragraphs from English to Japanese, emphasizing clear meaning and smooth flow.

Presentation Tips:

(7) Use *strategic pauses* to gather your thoughts and maintain a steady pace during translation.

(8) *Position yourself appropriately* within the group to ensure everyone can see and hear you clearly.

(9) *Control your facial expressions* to reflect the tone and meaning of the translated content accurately.

One-minute Talk
about International Interpreter Associations

Hello, everyone!

International *interpreter associations* play a vital role in fostering collaboration, setting standards, and advancing professional development for interpreters worldwide. Professional associations like AIIC uphold excellence in conference interpreting, while NAJIT supports judiciary interpreters and translators, ensuring quality standards in legal settings.

Academic associations such as IATIS and CLI contribute to research and scholarship in translation and interpreting studies, promoting interdisciplinary collaboration and fostering excellence in language services.

Locally, associations like VITIA in Vietnam advocate for high standards and ethical conduct among language professionals, enriching the professional landscape in their region. Consortiums like COTITT support educators and trainers in translation and interpreting, driving innovation and excellence in training programs globally.

Through networking, resources, and advocacy, these international interpreter associations play a crucial role in advancing professionalism, promoting ethical standards, and fostering continuous learning in the field of interpretation and translation.

Thank you!

Activity 1
Quick-response Vocabulary (Spoken)

To ***prepare to simultaneously interpret*** a groupmate's presentation about ***professional and academic interpreter associations***, give your bilingual vocabulary list to your partner who will interpret your presentation. Spend five minutes reviewing the words in both languages, and then practice ***quick-response vocabulary***. Here's how:

1. Your group member will read English words for you to say Japanese, then Japanese words for you say English, one after another.
2. Practice this for 5 to 7 minutes to improve your recall and speed.

Activity 2
Simultaneous Interpreting (Note-taking)

This activity simulates real-world simultaneous interpreting. You will use the presentations you have prepared about ***professional and academic interpreter associations*** to practice, focusing on capturing the speaker's message clearly and effectively.

1. In your groups, play the three-minute video presentations about ***professional and academic interpreter associations*** one by one.
2. The group member who practiced quick-response vocabulary will listen to the presentation with headphones and ***simultaneously interpret*** it aloud while everyone else watches.
3. If you have trouble while interpreting, quickly note down relevant words/phrases in the space below and provide a consecutive interpretation after the presentation.
4. Use the provided table to evaluate both your own and your group members' performance for improvement.

____

____

____

____

____

____

____

____

____

____

Evaluation Criteria	Rating (1-5)	Comments
Accuracy		Alignment with the original message
Clarity		Clarity of message delivery
Pronunciation		Pronunciation accuracy and clarity
Tone & Intonation		Matching speaker's tone and intonation
Pacing		Interpretation speed and flow
Confidence		Presenter's confidence and composure
Overall Performance		Overall interpretation evaluation

Preparation for Week 14

Task 1: Shadowing

Practice shadowing daily for 10-15 minutes, using materials like those on the **Bilingual News** website. Consistent shadowing habits will enhance language fluency and pronunciation.

Task 2: 3-Minute English PowerPoint Presentation

Prepare a 3-minute English presentation about the ***roles played by translators and interpreters at international film and animation festivals***, focusing on festivals in Japan and worldwide featuring Japanese films:

Instructions:

Your presentation should focus on the roles of translators and interpreters at international film and animation festivals, highlighting the importance of linguistic and cultural mediation in the global film industry.

Key Points to Cover:

1. Explain the essential roles of translators and interpreters at film festivals.
2. Explore the significance of their work in bridging linguistic and cultural gaps.
3. Provide examples of international film festivals in Japan that showcase foreign films and animations.
4. Identify prominent global festivals that have featured Japanese films and animations.

Hints and Research Guidance:

Research International Film Festivals in Japan:

- Look into renowned film festivals in Japan such as the Tokyo International Film Festival and the Hiroshima International Animation Festival.
- Investigate how these festivals promote international cultural exchange and the role of translators and interpreters in facilitating this exchange.

Explore Festivals Worldwide Featuring Japanese Films:

- Research major international film festivals like Cannes, Berlinale, Annecy, Venice Film Festival, and others that have showcased Japanese films.
- Pay attention to the recognition and awards Japanese films have received at these festivals, highlighting their global impact.

Understand Translator and Interpreter Roles:

- Learn about the duties of translators in subtitling and dubbing foreign films and animations for international audiences.
- Explore how interpreters provide live translation at film festivals during interviews, Q&A sessions, and panel discussions.

Emphasize Cultural Mediation:

- Highlight the importance of cultural mediation by translators and interpreters in conveying subtle nuances and context to diverse audiences.

- Discuss how translators and interpreters help foster cross-cultural understanding and appreciation in the film industry.

The following links include some useful information:

Tokyo International Film Festival	Hiroshima International Film Festival
https://tiff-jp.net/ja/	http://hiff.jp/
Hiroshima Animation Season	UNIJAPAN
https://hiroshimafest.org/	https://www.unijapan.org/

Record and export your presentation in .mp4 format for file sharing with your classmates in Week 14.

Task 3: Short Bilingual Vocabulary List

Generate a bilingual key vocabulary list (English and Japanese) for your PowerPoint presentation. Your classmates will utilize this list to prepare for Week 14 simultaneous interpretation tasks.

International Film Festivals

Warm-up 1
Consecutive Interpreting (Note-taking)

Listen to your teacher read the ***third episode*** of ***Secret's of the Fox's Ledger*** (Appendix D6.3) in three parts. Check the meaning of the following vocabulary/phrases before starting.

- **Part 7:** Possessed / Lamented / Ginzan Rat Poison
- **Part 8:** Secluded / Odd behavior / Fretted / Elusive creature / Ledger / Vanished / Confront / Affectionately / Patted / Spiritual / Mention / Encounter / Unresponsive
- **Part 9:** Crept / Moonlit / Pagoda / Intriguing figure / Engaging / Late-night rendezvous / Enigmatic / Puzzled / Baffled / Rebuke / Distressed / Suspecting / Sought / Spiritual intervention / Culminating / Deceased / Sense of closure / Swiftly / Hailed as a hero / Feat / Esteemed / Estate

INSTRUCTIONS:

1. Listen attentively as your teacher reads each part of the story.
2. Visualize the story in your mind as you hear it and take notes to help you remember the key points.
3. After each part, your teacher will pause. Use your notes to retell the story in Japanese to one of your classmates.

Warm-up 2
Shadowing (Prosody and Content)

Practice *prosody* and *content shadowing* using **Bilingual News**.

1. Use the QR code provided to access the latest bilingual talk on the **Bilingual News** website.
2. When the presenters speak English, *prosody shadow in English*; when they speak in Japanese, *prosody shadow in Japanese* (5 minutes). While doing this, solve the ten <u>simple arithmetic</u> questions on the next page.
3. Start over from the beginning of the presentation and practice *content shadowing*, taking notes in the space below the arithmetic questions on what the presenters are saying.

Bilingual News
https://bilingualnews.jp/podcastpage/

Ten Arithmetic Questions

(1) What is 29 + 18?	(6) Add 6.4 and 3.6.
(2) Subtract 52 from 116.	(7) Find the product of 11 and 13.
(3) Multiply 9 by 7.	(8) Subtract 86 from 150.
(4) Divide 81 by 9.	(9) Divide 56 by 4.
(5) Calculate 7 squared.	(10) What is 12% of 250?

Warm-up 3
Slash Reading and Sight Translation

The following is a short talk about *international film and animation festivals*. Before you start, double-check any words you need to confirm the Japanese translations for.

Slash Reading (90 Seconds):

- As you read the text, mark each significant pause or break with a slash (/) at points like commas, periods, or between phrases where you would naturally pause in speech.

Sight Translation (Five Minutes):

- In groups of two to three, take turns translating paragraphs from English to Japanese, emphasizing clear meaning and smooth flow.

Presentation Tips:

(10) Stay *relaxed and composed* to exude confidence and authority while conveying the translated content effectively.

(11) If you are unsure about a word or phrase, *use context clues* or make a quick decision to keep the translation moving.

(12) *Involve the audience* by making *eye contact, using gestures, and encouraging questions or feedback*.

Ninety-second Talk about International Film and Animation Festivals

Hello, everyone!

At *international film and animation festivals*, translators and interpreters play multifaceted roles vital to the success and inclusivity of these global events.

Translators support festival accessibility by subtitling films, translating written materials like program guides and scripts, and localizing festival websites for diverse audiences. Their work ensures that attendees from around the world can engage with film content and festival information seamlessly.

Interpreters, on the other hand, navigate real-time communication challenges during festival events. On-stage interpreters facilitate dialogue during film screenings, interviews, and award ceremonies, enabling international guests and audiences to engage with filmmakers and artists across language barriers.

Behind the scenes, interpreters act as artist liaisons, supporting filmmaker interactions with event organizers and the media. They provide technical interpreting for discussions on film production, animation techniques, and industry trends, fostering international engagement and collaboration.

VIP hospitality interpreters enhance the festival experience for guests, providing seamless communication for celebrities, jury members, and industry professionals. Their work ensures that all participants feel welcomed and valued throughout the event.

Through their diverse roles, translators and interpreters contribute to the cultural richness, accessibility, and global reach of International

Film and Animation Festivals, bridging linguistic barriers and fostering connections among audiences and creators from around the world.

Their indispensable efforts elevate the festival experience, fostering cross-cultural understanding and appreciation for diverse cinematic experiences on an international stage.

Thank you.

Activity 1
Quick-response Vocabulary (Spoken)

To **prepare to simultaneously interpret** a groupmate's presentation about **international film/animation festivals**, give your bilingual vocabulary list to your partner who will interpret your presentation. Spend five minutes reviewing the words in both languages, and then practice **quick-response vocabulary**. Here's how:

1. Your group member will read English words for you to say Japanese, then Japanese words for you say English, one after another.
2. Practice this for 5 to 7 minutes to improve your recall and speed.

Activity 2
Simultaneous Interpreting (Note-taking)

This activity simulates real-world simultaneous interpreting. You will use the presentations you have prepared about *international film/animation festivals* to practice, focusing on capturing the speaker's message clearly and effectively.

1. In your groups, play the three-minute video presentations about *international film/animation festivals* one by one.
2. The group member who practiced quick-response vocabulary will listen to the presentation with headphones and *simultaneously interpret* it aloud while everyone else watches.
3. If you have trouble while interpreting, quickly note down relevant words/phrases in the space below and provide a consecutive interpretation after the presentation.
4. Use the provided table to evaluate both your own and your group members' performance for improvement.

____

____

____

____

____

____

____

____

____

____

____

____

____

____

____

____

____

____

____

____

____

Evaluation Criteria	Rating (1-5)	Comments
Accuracy		Alignment with the original message
Clarity		Clarity of message delivery
Pronunciation		Pronunciation accuracy and clarity
Tone & Intonation		Matching speaker's tone and intonation
Pacing		Interpretation speed and flow
Confidence		Presenter's confidence and composure
Overall Performance		Overall interpretation evaluation

Preparation for Week 15

Task 1: Shadowing

Practice shadowing daily for 10-15 minutes, using materials like those on the **Bilingual News** website. Consistent shadowing habits will enhance language fluency and pronunciation.

Task 2: Review

Review what you have learned over the past four weeks.

Simultaneous Interpreting Review

Summary of Learning

Welcome to the third and final review lesson. Over the past four weeks, you have developed your interpreting skills in several key areas:

(1) *Audience Engagement in Sight Translation* - You have learned and practiced techniques to effectively *engage your audience* during sight translation exercises.

(2) *Slash Reading* and *Sight Translation* - You have used *slash reading* techniques to break down the three following short talks into manageable chunks to facilitate smoother and more accurate *sight translation*:

- When and where interpreters use sight translation
- Interpreter qualifications, international interpreter associations
- International film and animation festivals.

(3) *Consecutive Interpreting (Note-taking)* - You have practiced consecutive interpreting using translated and adapted stories by Kotaro Tanaka, with the aid of a vocabulary list to *expand your lexicon*.

(4) ***Prosody Shadowing*** - You have refined your prosody and content comprehension through shadowing exercises while taking notes using a ***bilingual podcast***, preparing you for more complex interpreting tasks.

(5) ***Knowledge about the Field of Interpreting*** - You have deepened your understanding about field of interpreting through presentations on:

- Companies/organizations recruiting English language specialists
- Interpreter qualifications and standards
- Professional and academic interpreter associations
- The varying roles of interpreters at international film and animation festivals.

(6) ***Quick-Response Vocabulary Tasks*** - You have transitioned from written to ***verbal quick-response vocabulary tasks***, developing the ability to swiftly and accurately respond in spoken language.

(7) ***Simultaneous Interpreting*** - You have practiced simultaneously interpreting your classmates' presentations on interpreting-related topics, ***sharpening your real-time translation skills***.

This review lesson will focus is on:

- Reviewing and assessing the effectiveness of what you've learned.
- Engaging in a short ***simultaneous interpreting (note-taking)*** test in front of your classmates to showcase your progress.

Learning Comprehension Check

(You can find the answers to these questions in the sight translation readings. Write your answers in English or Japanese.)

(1) In which settings do interpreters use sight translation to facilitate discussions at conferences and meetings?

____

____

____

(2) What types of documents do interpreters commonly sight translate in legal contexts?

____

____

____

(3) How do interpreters assist in educational environments?

____

____

____

(4) Which organization offers certifications for conference interpreters in diplomatic settings?

____

____

____

(5) What is the role of the CIOL certification for interpreters in the UK?

____

____

____

(6) Which organizations provide certifications for healthcare interpreters in the US, and how do these certifications impact their role?

____

____

____

(7) Which association upholds excellence in conference interpreting?

____

____

____

(8) What is the role of NAJIT in the legal field?

____

____

____

(9) How do academic associations like IATIS and CLI contribute to the field of interpreting and translation?

____

____

____

(10) How do translators contribute to the accessibility of international film and animation festivals?

____

____

____

(11) What roles do interpreters play during on-stage events at these festivals?

____

____

____

(12) How do VIP hospitality interpreters enhance the festival experience for guests?

____

____

____

Shadowing Review

Over the past four weeks, you have done four *prosody* and *content shadowing* exercises with segments from **Bilingual News**. Use the space on the following page to answer the following questions in English or Japanese:

(1) How has bilingual shadowing activities while doing a secondary task (arithmetic) improved your ability to shadow accurately?

(2) What, if any, impact has shadowing practice had on your ability to simultaneously interpret?

(3) How often have you practiced shadowing outside of class?

(4) What materials have you used for practicing shadowing outside of class?

(5) What steps can you take to further improve your shadowing technique?

Sight Translation Delivery Review

From Week 11 onward, you have learned *twelve presentation tips* designed to enhance your *sight translation delivery*. Use the space below to describe each tip in *Japanese*. Explain which you found to be the most effective and why.

Slash Reading and Sight Translation Review

Compare your answers to the following *slash reading* and *sight translation* questions with those you wrote in Week 10 to assess you progress.

(1) *Strengths and Weaknesses*: What are your strengths and weaknesses with sight translation?
(2) *Preparation Time*: How long did it take you to prepare for sight translating the short talks in this part of the course?

____

____

____

____

____

____

____

____

____

Simultaneous Interpreting Review

Your classmates have provided feedback on your *simultaneous interpreting (note-taking)* in the following areas: *accuracy, clarity, pronunciation, tone & intonation, pacing, confidence,* and *overall performance*. Reflect on your progress and the feedback you have received to answer the following questions in English or Japanese:

(1) What do you consider to be your *simultaneous interpreting strengths and weaknesses*?
(2) How do you intend to *enhance your simultaneous interpreting* performance from now on?

____

____

____

____

____

____

____

____

____

____

____

Simultaneous Interpreting Test

(Note-taking)

Part 1: 15-Minute Quick-Response Vocabulary Warm-up

Your teacher will assign you a test partner. Exchange your bilingual vocabulary lists for one of the following presentations (Choose the presentation you performed best on):

- Companies/organizations recruiting English language specialist
- Interpreter qualifications and standards
- Professional and academic interpreter associations
- The varying roles of interpreters at international film and animation festivals

You have fifteen minutes to practice *quick-response vocabulary (verbal/spoken)* with your test partner.

Part 2: Simultaneous Interpreting Performance

The mp4 presentations you selected will be played to the class. When it is time for your test partner's English presentation to be played, put on your headphones and ***simultaneously interpret*** it aloud while everyone else watches. If you have trouble while interpreting, remain calm and quickly note down relevant words/phrases in the space below. Then, provide a consecutive interpretation for those parts after the presentation. After you finish, evaluate your performance for improvement using the evaluation table, below.

Evaluation Criteria	Rating (1-5)	Comments
Accuracy		Alignment with the original message
Clarity		Clarity of message delivery
Pronunciation		Pronunciation accuracy and clarity
Tone & Intonation		Matching speaker's tone and intonation
Pacing		Interpretation speed and flow
Confidence		Presenter's confidence and composure
Overall Performance		Overall interpretation evaluation

Congratulations!

You've reached the end of *English-to-Japanese Interpreting 101*.

If you have any suggestions on how this text and the accompanying materials can be improved, or if you have requests for future courses, you can find contact details on the *Message from the Publisher* page.

Best of luck on your journey to becoming a world-class interpreter!

Week 1 Learning Review Quiz Answers

1. The mistake made by the interpreter was translating Nikita Khrushchev's phrase "My vas pokhoronim" as "We will bury you!" which led to a negative and threatening interpretation.
2. The incorrect translation heightened tensions between the Soviet Union and the US during the Cold War by creating a threatening image of Soviet intentions, potentially setting back East/West relations.
3. Accurate interpretation is crucial in diplomatic contexts to prevent misunderstandings, miscommunications, and conflicts that can arise from mistranslations.
4. Before simultaneous interpretation systems, interpreters worked mainly consecutively, pausing after speakers to provide translations and allowing a slower exchange of information.
5. The simultaneous interpretation system allows interpreters to translate a speaker's words instantly into a microphone as the speaker talks, providing seamless language translation for the audience in real-time, unlike the older method that had pauses between translations.
6. Interpreters develop their language skills by engaging in intensive training that includes shadowing, vocabulary expansion, and mastering unique techniques to effectively convey messages across different languages in conference settings.
7. Interpreters mentally prepare for high-pressure situations like the UN General Assembly by building glossaries, researching topics

extensively, reviewing previous talks, and supporting each other in a collaborative effort to ensure accurate and smooth interpretation amidst stressful environments.

Week 10 Learning Review Quiz Answers

1. Significant changes in translation technology over the past decade have been driven by artificial intelligence and machine learning.
2. Neural machine translation (NMT) is more effective than traditional methods because it considers entire sentences, making translations more accurate and fluent.
3. Real-time translation tools, integrated into communication platforms like email, messaging apps, and video conferencing, have revolutionized global business and collaboration by enabling multilingual communication and breaking down language barriers.
4. The two techniques discussed are Prosody Shadowing and Content Shadowing.
5. Activities like drawing or scribbling enhance focus, stimulate cognitive functions, improve concentration, and foster multitasking abilities, which are crucial for simultaneous interpreting.
6. Prosody and content shadowing add depth and nuance to interpretation, enhancing understanding and communication, and elevating the artistic aspects of interpretation when integrated with modern tools.
7. Chiune Sugihara issued transit visas to Jewish refugees fleeing Nazi-occupied Poland, despite strict instructions from his government, ultimately saving around 6,000 lives.
8. Chiune Sugihara hand-wrote over 2,000 visas over approximately four weeks in 1940.
9. Decades later, Chiune Sugihara was finally honored as one of the Righteous Among the Nations for his lifesaving work during World War II.

Week 15 Learning Review Quiz Answers

1. At conferences and meetings, interpreters use sight translation to translate documents and presentations to ensure seamless discussions.
2. In legal contexts, interpreters commonly sight translate legal documents such as contracts and reports during court proceedings and meetings with attorneys.
3. In educational environments, interpreters assist students with limited language proficiency by sight translating instructions, tests, and educational materials.
4. AIIC (International Association of Conference Interpreters) offers certifications for conference interpreters in diplomatic settings.
5. The CIOL (Chartered Institute of Linguists) certification ensures quality interpretation in legal settings internationally.
6. In the US, healthcare interpreters seek certifications from organizations like CCHI (Certification Commission for Healthcare Interpreters) and NBCMI (National Board of Certification for Medical Interpreters). These certifications provide critical language support in medical contexts.
7. AIIC (International Association of Conference Interpreters) upholds excellence in conference interpreting.
8. NAJIT (National Association of Judiciary Interpreters and Translators) supports judiciary interpreters and translators, ensuring quality standards in legal settings.
9. Academic associations such as IATIS (International Association for Translation and Intercultural Studies) and CLI (Critical Link International) contribute to research and scholarship in translation and interpreting studies, promoting interdisciplinary collaboration and fostering excellence in language services.
10. Translators contribute by subtitling films, translating written materials like program guides and scripts, and localizing festival

websites, ensuring attendees can engage with the content and information seamlessly.

11. On-stage interpreters facilitate dialogue during film screenings, interviews, and award ceremonies, enabling international guests and audiences to engage with filmmakers and artists across language barriers.

12. VIP hospitality interpreters enhance the festival experience by providing seamless communication for celebrities, jury members, and industry professionals, ensuring that all participants feel welcomed and valued throughout the event.

Example 90-Second Script

Aim for approximately 11 seconds per slide to maintain a smooth flow in your 90-second presentation.

TITLE SLIDE

Slide 1:

- Title: Exploring Ancient Roots of Interpreting in Japan
- By: Hina Tanaka

INTRODUCTION

Slide 2: Greetings and topic introduction

- Hello, everyone, I'm Hina Tanaka. Today, I will explore the ancient roots of interpreting in Japan during early trade relationships with neighboring countries.

MAIN CONTENT

Slide 3: 7th to 9th Centuries: (Timeline)

- During the 7th to 9th centuries, Japan engaged in trade with China and Korea, with figures like Shotoku Taishi fostering cultural exchanges between nations.

Slide 4: Trade Goods

- China and Korea traded luxury items like silk and tea with Japan.

Slide 5: Interpreters' Role:

- Interpreters, including notable figures such as Abe no Nakamaro, played a crucial role in facilitating trade negotiations.

Slide 6: Cultural Influence

- Early trade relationships led to significant cultural exchanges, impacting artistic and philosophical values.

CONCLUSION AND THANKS

Slide 7: Conclusion

- The early trade relationships fostered by interpreters between Japan, China, and Korea laid the groundwork for continued cultural and economic interactions in the region.

Slide 8: Thanks

- Thank you for joining me in exploring Japan's early trade relationships facilitated by interpreters.

Sample Bilingual Vocabulary List

1. Interpreting - 通訳
2. Ancient roots - 古代の起源
3. Trade relationships - 貿易関係
4. Neighboring countries - 隣接国
5. Fostering cultural exchanges - 文化交流を育む
6. Shotoku Taishi - 聖徳太子
7. Luxury items - 高級品
8. Silk - 絹
9. Tea - 茶
10. Abe no Nakamaro - 阿倍仲麻呂
11. Trade negotiations - 貿易交渉
12. Cultural influence - 文化的影響
13. Artistic values - 芸術的価値
14. Philosophical values - 哲学的価値
15. Economic interactions - 経済的交流

Kotaro Tanaka was born on March 2, 1880 in Misato Village, Nagaoka County, Kochi Prefecture (now Niida, Kochi City). His family once served as shipping agents for the Tosa clan.

After studying at a Chinese studies school and working as a substitute teacher and journalist for the Kochi Business Daily, Tanaka moved to Tokyo. From 1903 onward, he studied and wrote under the guidance of Keigetsu Omachi, Katai Tayama and Reiun Taoka, aiding their writing efforts. He was also associated with Shūsu Kōtoku. In 1909, Tanaka wrote most of Taoka's last work, *Meiji Hanshin Den* (lit.: Meiji Rebel Biography). Then, after Kotoku's execution in the High Treason Incident, he penned *Shūsu Sensei no Insho* (lit.: Impressions of Shūsu-sensei). Reflecting on his involvement, he noted that he could have been implicated himself.

Tanaka's debut publication was *Shiki to Jinsei* (lit.: The Four Seasons and Life) in 1911. Then, in 1914, he published *Taoka Reiun, Kōtoku Shūsu, Okumiya Kenyu Oukaeroku* (lit.: Reminiscences of Reiun Taoka, Shūsu Kōtoku, and Kenyu Okumiya), gaining significant attention.

Tanaka's ghost tales brought him widespread recognition, appearing in the Chūō Kōron (lit.: Central Review) during the Taisho period. He focused on collecting and rewriting ghost stories, amassing around 500 such tales, frequently republished. He admired classical Chinese novels like *Hong Lou Meng* (lit.: Dream of the Red Chamber) and *Liaozhai Zhiyi* (lit.: Strange Stories from a Chinese Studio), some of which he translated freely. His notable works include the collection *Kotaro Kenbunroku* (lit.: Kotaro's Observations), the epic *Senpu Jidai* (lit.: Whirlwind Age), serialized for 530 issues from 1929, and the adaptations

Nihon Kaidan Zenshuu (lit.: The Complete Collection of Japanese Ghost Stories) and *Shina Kaidan Zenshuu* (lit.: The Complete Collection of Chinese Ghost Stories). He published over 50 books during his life, including works on the Analects and other sutras.

From August 1934, he led the Coterie Magazine *Hakurou Sha Gekkan Zuihitsu* (lit.: Hakuansha Monthly Essays), creating a platform for many up-and-coming writers. His pupils and friends included Masuji Ibuse, Shiro Ozaki, Norio Taoka, Tsuneo Tomita, and Jun Sakakiyama. Norio Taoka later managed the magazine, which released 45 issues in total coming to an end in October 1943.

Tanaka also compiled numerous local histories and Meiji Restoration documents. He wrote biographies of Yuko Hamaguchi and Kinmochi Saionji. In his 1932 essay *Roushin Tanaka Mitsuaki O* (lit.: Elder Statesman Mitsuaki Tanaka), published in the Chūō Kōron, he criticized Tanaka's *Ishin Fu'un Kaikoroku* (lit.: Memoirs of Restoration Storms) for embellishment, despite Tanaka's prominent role in the Restoration.

In 1939, Tanaka returned to Tosa to research a biography of Yuzo Hayashi but fell ill in February 1940. Despite finishing the biography, his health declined, and he died on February 1, 1941 near his birthplace. After his death, he was posthumously awarded the 3rd Kikuchi Kan Prize. Monuments in his honor stand at his birthplace and Katsurahama Beach. His belongings and documents are preserved in the Kochi Prefectural Library.

All six stories in this appendix were translated from the original works of Kotaro Tanaka (1880 - 1941) and subsequently adapted to suit the requirements of a *consecutive interpreting* (*memory* or *note-taking*) exercise.

(D1) The Mystery of the Old Fox

Part 1: The Journey of Shigen

Once upon a time, there was a monk named Shigen. He followed his spiritual beliefs very strictly, wore simple robes, and liked being alone in nature rather than inside temples.

One night, he traveled four kilometers east of Hoshu Castle. Under the bright moon, he decided to rest in a peaceful graveyard surrounded by tombstones. The moonlight made it easy to see everything around him.

As he glanced up, Shigen spotted a fox beneath a nearby tree. The fox, balancing a skull on its head, was acting very strangely, mimicking human gestures.

Shigen chuckled softly. "What a funny little fox," he said to himself.

Suddenly, the fox plucked a blade of grass, draped it over its body, and transformed into a beautiful young woman. Shigen watched in amazement.

Part 2: The Encounter with the Soldier

As Shigen was still processing what he had seen, the silence of the night was broken by a horse neighing. A soldier appeared, riding along the path.

"Who travels at this hour?" Shigen wondered aloud.

The soldier approached, and the fox-woman moved to the roadside, crying loudly.

The soldier dismounted and walked toward her. "Miss, why are you crying here by the road?" he asked kindly.

Through her tears, she replied, "I am from Ekishu. My husband died last year, leaving me with nothing. I am trying to return to my family, but it's getting late."

The soldier's heart softened. "If you don't mind, I can take you on my horse. It would be my pleasure to help you. No one should have to travel alone at night."

"Thank you, kind sir," said the fox-woman, hiding her joy.

Just as the soldier was about to lift her onto his horse, Shigen stepped forward and warned, "Be careful! This woman is not a woman; she is a fox in disguise."

Part 3: The Reveal

The soldier looked at Shigen angrily. "Monk, how dare you accuse her? She is in need."

Without getting angry, Shigen replied, "If you doubt me, I will show you the truth." He then started chanting a powerful mantra and waved his wooden staff. "Reveal your true form now, or face the consequences!"

The fox-woman began to twitch and twist in pain. The soldier watched in shock as she changed back into a fox. The fox fell to the ground, bleeding, and died.

The graveyard became silent again. The dead fox lay among the tombstones, surrounded by skull fragments and grass blades.

The soldier, both horrified and thankful, turned to Shigen and bowed deeply. "I am sorry for doubting you, wise monk. You saved me from a dangerous trick."

Shigen nodded. "We must always be careful of illusions that try to deceive us. This is a reminder that things are not always what they seem."

Together, they buried the fox's body and then went their separate ways, each taking with them a lesson about the mysterious forces in the world.

And so, the story of Shigen and the fox lived on, a tale told to remind people of the wisdom in being cautious and the ever-present danger of deception.

(D2) The Fable of the Fox and Racoon Dog

Part 1: The Journey Begins

Above the tomb of King Hui-o lived a fox and a raccoon dog. They weren't regular animals; both were over a thousand years old and had magic powers. One day, they heard about a smart and talented governor named Zhang. Curious, they decided to test themselves and cause some trouble. They transformed into young scholars and rode off on horseback.

As they approached the city gates, a guardian stopped them.

"Where are you going?" the guardian asked.

"We're going to talk with Zhang," the raccoon dog said confidently.

"Be careful," the guardian warned. "Zhang is very wise, and I worry about what you might do."

But the raccoon dog and the fox didn't listen. They continued on their journey without hesitation.

Part 2: The Debate with Zhang

When they reached Zhang's home, the disguised fox and raccoon dog started a debate with him. They were clever and managed to make the great governor uneasy.

Seeing how unusual they were, Zhang grew suspicious. He turned to his advisor, Lei, who had just arrived.

"These two scholars seem strange to me," Zhang said. "What should we do?"

"Let's bring in the dogs. They might show us the true nature of these visitors," Lei suggested.

Zhang agreed and brought in the dogs. Despite this, the fox and raccoon dog stayed calm.

"Our wisdom comes from the heavens," the raccoon dog said proudly.

Part 3: Revealing the Truth

Thinking about the situation, Zhang said, "A spirit that is a hundred years old can be revealed by dogs, but a demon that is a thousand years old only shows itself when exposed to the flames of a sacred tree that has lived for a millennium."

"Where can we find such a tree?" Lei asked.

"The ancient tree by the tomb of King Hui-o has lived for a thousand years," Zhang replied.

Zhang sent a messenger to get the tree. When he arrived at the tree, a child in a blue kimono appeared in the sky and questioned the messenger.

"Where are you from?" the child asked sadly. "The old raccoon dog acted foolishly, didn't he? He refused to listen to my warnings, leading to this disaster."

Despite the child's sorrow, the messenger cut down the tree. Blood flowed from it when it was cut. Then, when the tree was set on fire, the true forms of the raccoon dog and the fox were revealed. Zhang quickly caught and punished them.

(D3) The Married Woman
and Her Mysterious Housemate

Part 1: The Missing Peddler

In the small village of Toyoda, there lived a traveling salesman named Nizo Kutsuzawa. Every day, he went to different villages to trade things. Nizo's wife, Nao, was very pretty and kind. She was liked by everyone in the village.

One cold day in February 1932, Nizo didn't come home like he usually did. Nao was very worried and searched everywhere for him, but he was nowhere to be found. Days went by, and still, there was no news of Nizo.

"Oh, where could Nizo be?" Nao's voice trembled with fear as she looked for him in every corner of the village.

Part 2: The Unexpected Return

When the snow melted in April, Nizo suddenly returned home. Nao was overjoyed and ran to him, tears of relief streaming down her face. "Nizo, you're back! I missed you so much," she exclaimed, hugging him tightly.

Nizo held her and said, "I'm here now, Nao. I missed you too."

Nizo shared stories of his long journeys and showed Nao the money he had earned, making her feel better. Nao smiled through her tears, happy to have Nizo back. Nizo promised her, "I'll come back home every evening from now on, so you don't need to worry."

Part 3: Intrusion and Revelation

One evening, while enjoying dinner together, their peaceful moment was interrupted. An intruder barged in, causing chaos. He broke the delicate doors and lashed out with a club. Nao's eyes widened in shock as she watched, fear gripping her heart.

"Who are you? Why are you here?" Nao's voice shook as she tried to make sense of the situation. The intruder attacked Nizo, and to Nao's surprise, the man who she thought was Nizo transformed into a raccoon dog before her eyes, leaving her bewildered and scared.

As the raccoon dog lay motionless on the floor, Nao looked at the intruder. It was Nizo. He spoke, "Nao, it's me. I don't know what happened, but I am here with you now."

Still reeling, Nao whispered softly, "What a strange and unexpected turn of events life has brought us." That evening, she fell ill and passed away.

(D4) The Raccoon Dog and the Haiku Poet

Part 1: The Enchanting Encounter

The peaceful village of Rendaiji, known for its sweet persimmons and the nearby Ise Grand Shrine, was home to Shozo Sawada. He was revered for his haikus, writing under the pen name Rokumei Shikanai. His poetic talents made him stand out.

One serene evening, while Shozo was enjoying his tea, a shadow caught his eye. "Well, now, who might you be?" he wondered aloud as he stepped outside. There, he found a raccoon dog joyfully looking up at him.

"Ah, aren't you a friendly one? Do you want something to eat?" Shozo's warm voice echoed in the crisp air as he shared his meal with the raccoon dog. This sparked an unexpected companionship that filled his home with newfound warmth.

Part 2: Bonds Beyond Words

As the days passed, the raccoon dog's visits became routine. Shozo's home was filled with a sense of shared comfort. When Shozo fell sick, he whispered a quiet plea to the raccoon dog, "Please, my friend, safeguard this space for us." With a mix of sadness and duty, the raccoon dog bid farewell as Shozo peacefully passed away.

The next day, a mysterious woman with tears in her eyes was seen near Shozo's resting place. "Who is she, and what brings her here?" the villagers whispered, curious about her unspoken connection. Amidst their whispers and nods, a silent promise formed among the village folk: they would honor the bond between Shozo, the raccoon dog, and nature.

Part 3: Echoes of Harmony

The stories of Shozo and the raccoon dog continued to circulate through Rendaiji, becoming cherished legends that taught the villagers the importance of living in harmony with nature. "Did you hear about the loyal raccoon dog that kept Shozo company?" a villager might ask, sparking curiosity and interest among the listeners.

The village, united by the memories of Shozo and the mysterious woman, embraced a deep respect for the interconnectedness of all living beings. These tales reminded future generations of the enduring bond between humans and the natural world.

Guided by the spirit of Shozo and his loyal raccoon dog, Rendaiji thrived. The villagers developed a profound appreciation for the beauty and tranquility of their surroundings, letting Shozo's legacy inspire them every day.

(D5) Mujina: The Mischievous Shape-Shifter of Kiinokuni Hill

Part 1: The Veiled Tears at Kikinokuni Hill

During the last days of the Edo period, Akindo, a respected merchant known for his keen eye for quality, walked near the mysterious Kiinokuni Hill in Akasaka. To his left was the tall wall of Kishu's residence, and to his right, the quiet water of the moat. Shadows from the dense grove of trees at the Hikone residence made the night feel eerie. The silence was broken only by the soft rustling of leaves.

Akindo noticed a figure by a willow tree next to the calm moat. It was a woman. Her face was hidden in her hands. She was crying softly.

Akindo approached her, stopping a short distance away. "What troubles you, my dear? Please, don't suffer alone," he said gently, extending a hand towards her.

The young woman continued to sob, her cries filling the moonlit night. Akindo, feeling a mix of empathy and curiosity, spoke again, "You don't have to be alone. Share your pain with me. What is wrong, my dear?"

The woman slowly lowered her hands. Her face was revealed, but it was featureless—no eyes, no nose, no mouth. The sight sent a chill down Akindo's spine.

Gasping in shock, Akindo took a step back and quickly moved away, heading up the hill. He hurried toward the warm lights of Yotsuya, where a small soba stall offered relief from the unsettling encounter.

Part 2: The Specter and the Soba Stall

Guided by a mix of fear and curiosity, Akindo sought refuge at the soba stall. He sought comfort in the familiar, trying to make sense of the strange encounter at Kiinokuni Hill. The elderly man at the stall noticed Akindo and nodded in acknowledgment.

"It's rare to see someone in such distress," the elderly man remarked. "What brought you to this humble stall in such a state?"

Taking a deep breath, Akindo began to explain the eerie encounter at Kiinokuni Hill. "I saw a woman crying, but... her face was featureless— no eyes, no nose, no mouth."

The old man's expression shifted slightly. "Such encounters are not unheard of," he said quietly, stirring the simmering broth. "There are often stories of spirits roaming our world, especially at night."

Akindo, still shaken, asked, "Do you know what it could mean?"

Leaning in, the elderly man responded thoughtfully, "The woman's tears might reveal more than just sorrow. What else did you sense in that moment?"

As the night air filled with the scent of simmering soba and the clinking of bowls, Akindo looked into the old man's eyes. In an instant, his eyes, nose and mouth vanished as his face became featureless.

Part 3: Unveiling the Tanuki's Mischief

The whispers of Akindo's supernatural encounter at Kiinokuni Hill spread quickly through the village. Stories of faceless maidens and ghostly beings filled the air, weaving fear and wonder among the villagers. Candles flickered in windows, casting dancing shadows as people spoke in hushed voices about the spirits that wandered the night.

One villager spoke up, "Did you hear about the maiden with no face? It's the talk of the village."

Another shivered, "I saw strange shadows near the hill last night. It felt like the spirits were close."

Villagers began to speak even more about the legend of the mischievous raccoon dog that roamed Kiinokuni Hill. Akindo's story became etched in their minds, a warning about the hidden forces between the world of mortals and the spirit realm.

(D6.1) Secrets of the Fox's Ledger (1)

Part 1: The Mysterious Awakening

In the final years of the Edo period, in a serene corner near Kikigaki Temple in Hongo, there lived a wandering merchant called Shinzaburo. One time, while Shinzaburo was away on a business trip, his wife, Otaki, their son, Shinichi, and the household manager, Chiyoko, found themselves facing an unexpected visitor.

The night air was crisp as Otaki settled into her slumber. Suddenly, a presence, a looming figure by her side, stirred her awake. Startled, she exclaimed, "Who are you? Wake up this instant!"

The mysterious man awoke with a fleeting smile before swiftly vanishing, leaving Otaki bewildered. Calling out for Chiyoko, she recounted the eerie encounter, "Chiyoko, there was a man. He vanished into thin air!"

Worried, Chiyoko searched the house meticulously, finding no trace of the intruder. As the night wore on, the sense of unease grew, shrouding the household in a veil of mystery.

Part 2: Shadows of Intrigue

In the soft hues of dawn, the peculiar events of the night lingered, casting a shadow over Otaki's demeanor. Feeling the weight of uncertainty, Shinichi whispered to Chiyoko about his concerns, "Chiyoko, did you see how Mother acted last night?"

Chiyoko replied, "Yes, quite strange indeed. We must remain alert."

As the next evening fell, the trio prepared for a night of vigilance. With doors slightly ajar and lanterns casting dim light, they awaited the unknown. Shinichi, restless and wary, muttered, "I hope Father returns soon."

A gentle touch from Chiyoko jolted Shinichi from his sleep, prompting a search for the elusive presence. Together, they found Otaki in a hidden corner of the house. On being found, she pushed past them, ran to the *tatami* room, and pulled the doors closed.

Part 3: Echoes of the Enigma

Hidden away in the *tatami* room, Otaki's words carried a weight of unknown intent, "No one is permitted enter." Shinichi and Chiyoko stood outside, their hearts racing with questions left unanswered.

In the stillness of the night, shadows danced as whispers of the enigma echoed through the house. Shinichi, consumed by thoughts of the inexplicable events, awaited the first light of dawn with a mix of trepidation and curiosity.

(D6.2) Secrets of the Fox's Ledger

Part 4: Shadows in the Morning Light

In the morning, Chiyoko cautiously entered the *tatami* room. Otaki was lost in thought, her head resting on folded arms.

Speaking softly to avoid startling her Otaki, Chiyoko gently inquired, "Hello, Ms. Otaki?"

Otaki, awakened from her sleep, scowled at Chiyoko, "Why are you disturbing me here? Go away."

Unfazed, Chiyoko replied, "I just wanted to see how you're feeling. Is everything alright?"

Annoyed, Otaki dismissed her, "You're bothering me. Please, leave."

Returning to the tea room, Chiyoko told Shinichi about her discussion with Otaki, who mused, "How peculiar. Mother's behavior really is quite unusual."

Throughout the day, Otaki remained sequestered, exhibiting distant and erratic behaviors that left Shinichi and Chiyoko puzzled.

Part 5: Echoes of the Hidden Realm

In the passing days, Otaki's seclusion deepened, signaling an ominous presence lurking within the household. Chiyoko and Shinichi discerned that there must be an unsettling energy at play, possibly linked to a malevolent force. "There is a dark energy at work in this house," Chiyoko said. "Perhaps it's a fox or racoon dog seeking to attach itself to your mother."

Deep in thought, Shinichi contemplated the mysterious origin of the hidden entity, pondering, "Could it be a fox that is living within the walls of our home?"

As a sense of foreboding enveloped them, Chiyoko and Shinichi prepared to stay vigilant, anticipating Shinzaburo's return and the resolution of the enigmatic events haunting their household.

Part 6: Whispers in the Night

The next night, armed with a dagger, Shinichi waited in the tea room. He was prepared to face any unknown creature lurking in the shadows.

When a dog-like creature appeared, Shinichi lunged at it, sinking his dagger into its side. To his surprise, Otaki's cries of distress reverberated through the house.

Reflecting on the meaning of the unearthly creature's presence within their home, Shinichi showed his blood stained dagger to Chiyoko. Peering at the dark-colored blood, Chiyoko whispered, "Shinichi, what have we done? Is this truly the malevolent force we anticipated, or have we mistaken a mere animal for something more sinister?"

Shinichi replied in a hushed tone, "I'm not sure, Chiyoko. There is something unnatural about this creature, yet its eyes held a glimmer of familiarity. Could it be a manifestation of a spirit bound by unfinished business, seeking solace within our home?"

(D6.3) Secrets of the Fox's Ledger

Part 7: Ginzan Rat Poison

Worried about his mother, Shinichi decided to visit his friend Yoshi to ask for his advice. Yoshi, who sold fish, was surprised to see him. "Hey, Shinichi! Long time no see. Where have you been?"

"I haven't hidden away at home because my mother was possessed by a fox," Shinichi explained.

"Really? A fox possessed her?" Yoshi asked, surprised.

"Yes, I even managed hurt it," Shinichi insisted.

"Wow, that's something. Foxes are so fast," Yoshi reacted.

"It got away. I wish I had caught it," Shinichi lamented.

"How about using Ginzan Rat Poison?" Yoshi suggested

"Good idea. I think I've got some at home," Shinichi replied, quickly getting up to return home.

Part 8: Revelations and Retreats

As the days turned into nights, Otaki stayed secluded, showing no odd behavior, while Shinichi fretted about the elusive creature. Thoughts of the dagger and Ginzan Rat Poison troubled him.

One evening when Shinichi was walking past the temple adjacent to his house, he spotted a dog-like creature resting on a large stone reading in a ledger. On hearing Shinichi's footsteps, it vanished, leaving the ledger behind.

Shinichi picked up the ledger and flicked through the pages. He stopped on the middle page. His mother's was written in bold ink with a circle around it. He decided to confront and kill the fox.

On returning home, Shinichi found his father, Shinzaburo, talking to Chiyoko.

"Welcome home, Father," he said.

"Oh, Shinichi. It's good to see you."

After hearing about Otaki's worrying behavior and Shinichi's brave actions, Shinzaburo affectionately patted his son's head. "You did well, son," he said. "It seems like your mother might need some spiritual help. I'll deal with it now."

Nodding silently, Shinichi decided not to mention his encounter with fox and its ledger to his father.

"Let's go check on her?" Shinzaburo suggested, leading the way to the front *tatami* room. Otaki lay still. She was unresponsive to Shinzaburo's questions. Her silence showed no signs of improvement.

Deciding to let Otaki rest, Shinzaburo, Shinichi, and Chiyoko moved to the tea room.

"She's a bit better now," Chiyoko said.

"Really? How?" Shinzaburo asked.

"She looks at us now, albeit momentarily," Chiyoko explained.

Part 9: Dawn of Resolutions

Shinichi crept into the moonlit temple pagoda after dark, armed with a hidden dagger and Ginzan Rat Poison. An intriguing figure, a young man with painted lips, settled nearby, engaging in a mysterious late-night rendezvous. Shinichi's watched closely but could not hear what they were saying.

Their enigmatic conversation continued over a meal, leaving Shinichi feeling puzzled. He crept closer, noticing a basket full of fish on a rock behind the two men. He carefully scattering the Ginzan Rat Poison on the fish and returned home.

A peaceful night passed for Otaki. The following morning, Shinzaburo discovered a deceased fox at the entrance to the house, bringing a sense of closure. Otaki's recovery followed swiftly, and Shinichi was hailed a hero for his bravery, earning him an invitation to the esteemed Hatamoto family estate.

Business Interpreter (Example)

Interpreter Skills and Sub-skills

Core Skills

- English Language Proficiency
- Consecutive Interpreting (Memory)
- Consecutive Interpreting (Note-taking)
- Simultaneous Interpreting
- Broadcast Interpreting
- Sight Translation

Sub-skills

- Note-taking
- Shadowing
- Slash Reading

Interpreter Knowledge

- History/Background of Interpreting
- Types of Interpreters
- Types of Interpreting
- Interpreter Training Techniques
- Note-taking Techniques
- Interpreter Technology/Tools
- Recruiters of Interpreters
- Recruiters of English Specialists
- Interpreter Qualifications
- Interpreter Associations
    - Professional
    - Academic

Domain Specific Knowledge/Qualifications

- Business Knowledge and Terminology
- Bookkeeping
- Secretarial
- Project Management
- Cultural Awareness
- Industry Specific Terminology
- Negotiation Skills
- Interpersonal Communication Skills
- Ethical Guidelines and Professional Conduct
- Presentation Skills
- Technical Terminology

Situational Knowledge

- Knowledge about how to prepare for an interpreter task (Pre-task Research and Training)
- Knowledge about which interpreter skills to use in specific situations and how to use them

- *Adaptation*: The process of altering content to fit a different cultural or linguistic context while retaining the original message and intent. Unlike localization, adaptation may involve significant changes to the content to make it more relevant and engaging for the target audience.
- *Back Translation*: The practice of translating a translated document back into the original language by a different translator to check for accuracy and consistency, often used in the quality assurance process.
- *Braille Translation*: The conversion of written text into Braille, a tactile writing system used by individuals who are visually impaired, ensuring accessibility to written content.
- *Broadcast Interpreting*: Interpreting that is done for live broadcasts, such as news programs, where accuracy and immediacy are crucial.
- *Certified Interpreter*: An interpreter who has completed formal training, passed certification exams, and meets specific standards set by professional associations or regulatory bodies to ensure competency and professionalism in the field.
- *Community Interpreting*: Interpreting services offered in community settings such as schools, social services, or immigration offices to aid non-English speakers in accessing essential services.
- *Computer-assisted Translation (CAT) Tools*: Software programs that assist translators in the translation process by storing translations, suggesting terminology, and offering features for collaboration and consistency across projects.

- *Conference Interpreting*: Interpreting services provided at conferences, seminars, or large-scale events to facilitate communication among participants speaking different languages.
- *Consecutive Interpreting (Memory)*: The skill of interpreting spoken language consecutively from one language to another by relying on memory, without the aid of notes.
- *Consecutive Interpreting (Note-taking)*: The skill of interpreting spoken language consecutively by taking notes to aid in accurately conveying the message once the speaker finishes.
- *Cultural Mediation*: The process of interpreting and explaining cultural nuances, customs, and behaviors to bridge communication gaps between individuals from different cultural backgrounds during interpreting assignments.
- *Deaf-Blind Interpreting*: Specialized interpreting services that use tactile sign language or other methods of communication to assist individuals who are both deaf and blind, ensuring they can receive and convey information effectively.
- *Domain Knowledge*: Understanding of a specific area beyond just language, like knowing business or medical terms, which helps interpreters communicate complex ideas accurately.
- *English Language Proficiency*: The ability to understand, speak, read, and write in English fluently and accurately, a crucial skill for interpreters working in English-speaking environments.
- *Guide Interpreting*: A type of interpreting where the interpreter accompanies a visitor or group of visitors, providing on-the-spot interpretation in a touristic or informal setting.
- *Interpreter Fatigue*: The physical and mental exhaustion that interpreters experience due to prolonged periods of intense concentration and effort required in interpreting tasks, which can affect performance and accuracy.
- *Interpreter Knowledge*: Information interpreters have about interpreting, including its history, types of interpreters, and training techniques they need to know to do their job well.

- *Interpreter Skills*: Abilities like speaking multiple languages fluently and interpreting conversations accurately.
- *Interpreter Sub-skills*: Smaller abilities like note-taking or quickly reading and understanding written text that help interpreters do their job better.
- *Interpreting*: Changing spoken or signed words from one language into another in real-time, happening during events like meetings and conferences.
- *Interpreting Equipment*: Devices and tools used by interpreters to facilitate communication, such as interpreting booths, headsets, microphones, and audio systems, essential for conferences and large events.
- *Interpreting Ethics*: Guidelines and principles that interpreters follow to ensure professionalism, confidentiality, impartiality, and accuracy in their interpreting services, particularly in sensitive or high-stakes situations.
- *Interpreting Modes*: Different ways in which interpreters provide interpretation, such as simultaneous, consecutive, whispering, liaison, or escort interpreting, each suited for specific communication contexts and settings.
- *Legal Interpreting*: Interpreting that takes place in legal settings such as courtrooms, police stations, or law firms, where accurate language translation is crucial for legal proceedings.
- *Liaison Interpreting*: A type of interpreting where the interpreter facilitates communication between two individuals or small groups who speak different languages, often in informal settings like business meetings or social gatherings.
- *Localization*: Adapting translated content to suit the linguistic, cultural, and technical requirements of a specific target audience or region, ensuring that the content resonates with the local audience.
- *Machine Translation*: The automatic translation of text or speech from one language to another using computer algorithms and

technology, often used for quick translations but may lack the nuance and accuracy of human translation.

- *Machine-assisted Human Translation*: A translation workflow in which human translators use machine translation tools to generate initial drafts, which they then edit and refine to ensure high quality and accuracy.

- *Medical Interpreting*: Interpreting in healthcare settings to assist communication between healthcare providers and patients who speak different languages, ensuring accurate and culturally appropriate care.

- *Natural Language Processing (NLP)*: A branch of artificial intelligence that focuses on the interaction between computers and human language, enabling tasks like text translation, sentiment analysis, and language generation.

- *Note-taking*: The ability to take effective and structured notes to aid in the interpreting process, enhancing memory and accuracy.

- *Post-editing*: The process of reviewing and correcting machine translations by human translators to improve quality, accuracy, and fluency levels, commonly used in conjunction with machine translation for efficiency.

- *Public Service Interpreting*: Interpreting services provided in public sector settings such as healthcare, legal, and social services, ensuring non-native speakers can access essential services and information.

- *Quality Assurance*: Processes and procedures followed by translators and interpreters to ensure the accuracy, consistency, and quality of their work, often involving proofreading, editing, and feedback mechanisms.

- *Relay Interpreting*: An interpreting method where the message is interpreted from the source language to an intermediary language and then from that intermediary language to the target language, often used when direct interpretation between two languages is not available.

- ***Remote Interpreting***: Interpreting that is conducted over a digital platform, such as video conferencing or phone calls, without the interpreter and speakers being in the same physical location.
- ***Remote Simultaneous Interpreting***: Similar to remote interpreting, this term specifically refers to simultaneous interpreting conducted remotely using digital platforms and specialized software to provide real-time interpretation.
- ***Shadowing***: The technique of repeating what is being said by a speaker in real-time to improve language comprehension and interpretation skills.
- ***Sight Translation***: The skill of reading a text in one language and orally translating it into another language in real-time, typically useful for written documents or texts.
- ***Simultaneous Interpreting***: The ability to interpret spoken language simultaneously while the speaker is talking, often used in conference settings where real-time interpretation is required.
- ***Situational Knowledge***: Knowing how to prepare for interpreting tasks, which skills to use in different situations, and how to adjust communication based on the context to make interpreting smoother and clearer.
- ***Slash Reading***: The practice of reading quickly and efficiently, often used in interpreting to grasp the main points of a text without reading every word.
- ***Terminology Management***: The process of creating and maintaining glossaries and terminology databases to ensure consistent and accurate interpretation of specialized terms across different interpreting assignments.
- ***Terminology Management Systems (TMS)***: Specialized software used to create, store, and manage a repository of terms and their translations, ensuring consistency and accuracy across translation projects.
- ***Transcreation***: A form of translation that involves creatively adapting content from one language to another while maintaining the

original intent, style, and emotional impact, often used for marketing and advertising materials.

- *Translation*: Changing written text from one language into another while keeping the original meaning.

- *Translation Memory*: A database or software tool that stores previously translated segments or phrases, enabling translators to reuse and maintain consistency in translations, especially in technical or repetitive content.

- *Translation Software*: Computer programs designed to aid translators in the process of converting text from one language to another, providing features like translation suggestions, terminology management, and formatting tools to enhance efficiency and accuracy.

- *Voiceover Translation*: The process of recording a translated script over the original audio of a video or film, allowing the audience to hear the translation while still perceiving the original speech's tone and intonation.

- *Whispered Interpreting*: A form of simultaneous interpreting where the interpreter whispers a translation to the listener while the speaker continues to talk. This method is useful in situations where only one or a few individuals require translation in a group setting.

Matatabi Press is always looking for new talent. If you fall into any of the following categories, please contact us at <u>press@matatabi-japan.com</u>:

- A writer interested in sharing your story with the world
- An EFL/ESL professional passionate about creating English graded readers
- A Japanese language specialist looking to collaborate on a Japanese graded reader
- A Japanese-English translator eager to translate Japanese literature
- A language studies, translation, or interpreting specialist looking to publish your research or a textbook

Get in touch with us and become a part of our growing team.

John McLean (Emcee/Interpreter: far left) at the opening of Hiroshima International Film Festival 2022

John McLean, a British-born Japanese-English translator and interpreter, is esteemed as one of Japan's premier interpreters. In addition to his roles as a production editor, emcee, film festival talk-show host, and associate professor at a university in Hiroshima, his interpretation skills stand out. His diverse clientele includes renowned Japanese athletes like Ai Fukuhara (table tennis player) and Kohei Uchimura (gymnast), esteemed personalities such as Nana Komatsu (actor/model) and Kentaro Sakaguchi (actor), as well as dignitaries like Kazumi Matsui (Mayor of Hiroshima). He has also collaborated with major media outlets like NBC, CBC, and Al Jazeera. Apart from his interpreting expertise, his translation, subtitling, and editing projects with Japanese film directors and dedication to fostering emerging filmmakers at the Berlin Film Festival demonstrate his significant impact on the Japanese film industry.